CHINA

THE WASHINGTON PAPERS

... intended to meet the need for an authoritative, yet prompt, public appraisal of the major developments in world affairs.

Series Editor: Walter Laqueur

Managing Editor: Donna R. Spitler

MANUSCRIPT SUBMISSION

The Washington Papers and Praeger Publishers welcome inquiries concerning manuscript submissions. Please include with your inquiry a curriculum vitae, synopsis, table of contents, and estimated manuscript length. Manuscript length must fall between 30,000 and 45,000 words. All submissions will be peer reviewed. Submissions to *The Washington Papers* should be sent to *The Washington Papers*, Center for Strategic and International Studies, 1800 K Street NW, Washington, DC 20006. Book proposals should be sent to Praeger Publishers, 88 Post Road West, P.O. Box 5007, Westport, CT 06881-5007.

THE WASHINGTON PAPERS/182

AGING CHINA

The Demographic Challenge to China's Economic Prospects

Robert Stowe England
Foreword by Pieter Bottelier

Published with the Center for Strategic
and International Studies, Washington, D.C.

PRAEGER

Westport, Connecticut
London

Library of Congress Cataloging-in-Publication Data

England, Robert Stowe.
   Aging China : the demographic challenge to China's economic prospects / Robert Stowe England ; foreword by Pieter Bottelier.
      p. cm. — (The Washington papers ; 182)
   "Published with the Center for Strategic and International Studies, Washington, D.C."
   Includes bibliographical references and index.
   ISBN 0–275–98683–7 (alk. paper) — ISBN 0–275–98684–5
   1. Older people—Government policy—China. 2. Age distribution (Demography)—Economic aspects—China. 3. China—Population—Economic aspects. I. Center for Strategic and International Studies (Washington, D.C.) II. Title. III. Series.
HQ1064.C6E54 2005
305.26′0951—dc22   2004025261

The Washington Papers are written under the auspices of the Center for Strategic and International Studies (CSIS) and published with CSIS by Praeger Publishers. CSIS, as a public policy research institution, does not take specific policy positions. Accordingly, all views, positions, and conclusions expressed in the volumes of this series should be understood to be solely those of the authors.

British Library Cataloguing-in-Publication Data is available.

Library of Congress Catalog Card Number: 2004025261
ISBN: 0–275–98683–7 (cloth)
        0–275–98684–5 (paper)

First published in 2005

Praeger Publishers, 88 Post Road West, Westport, CT 06881
An imprint of Greenwood Publishing Group, Inc.
www.praeger.com
Printed in the United States of America

The paper used in this book complies with the Permanent Paper Standard issued by the National Information Standards Organization (Z39.48-1984).

10 9 8 7 6 5 4 3 2 1

Contents

Foreword

Pieter Bottelier

The story of aging's impact on China takes place within the larger context of global aging. Although the average age of most populations of the world is rising, China is aging faster than most countries.

This volume—Robert England's fourth on the topic of aging—is another milestone in the ongoing work of the Global Aging Initiative at the Center for Strategic and International Studies in Washington, D.C. When the initiative got under way in 1999, its focus was on the impact of aging in developed nations on government spending, benefits for the elderly, the economy, and on financial markets. Upon completion of the original project, the Global Aging Initiative set out to explore the potential impact of aging on China, the world's largest developing country.

China's economy has developed extremely fast during the past quarter century. Although the average per capita income—around $1,000 in 2003—is still very modest, it is likely that China will become a lower middle income country in the next few decades. The rapid aging of its population, however, may set China on a different course from that of the developed nations or even the Asian Tigers—South Korea, Taiwan, Hong Kong, and Singapore. A different course is indicated, because China's aging started at a much earlier stage of development than in Europe,

Pieter Bottelier, former chief of the Beijing Office for the World Bank, is associate professor of China studies at the Johns Hopkins University.

Japan, and other Asian countries. By 2040 China will have a higher average age than the United States.

The impact of aging presents enormous challenges for the Chinese government in its efforts to steer the nation through its transition to a market economy and orderly integration into the global economy. China's internal development and role on the global stage will be strongly influenced by the aging process and the way in which the economic and social consequences of this process will be managed.

After serving as director of research for CSIS's Global Aging Initiative from 1999 to 2001, Robert England set out to examine the impact of aging in China in 2002. His background—as publisher of a series of research papers and author of three books on the impact of aging on developed nations, the global economy, and world financial markets—uniquely qualified him to tackle the subject. His research brought him to the conclusion that, over the long term, demographics will probably influence China's economic development and reform efforts more strongly than any other factor.

This volume addresses the challenges that lie ahead for China by reviewing the effects of aging on several major areas of national life. They include the ongoing retrenchment in benefits for employees of state-owned enterprises under what used to be the "Iron Rice Bowl" system in earlier years, before market reforms became serious. Other areas include the changing social security system and the difficult task of balancing rapid development while preserving a level of benefits and social security that will preserve stability during transition.

England assesses the factors driving China's transition to a market economy and the financial burdens weighing on the government as it manages a series of simultaneous transitions—for example, the legacy costs of China's generous old system of pension benefits and the large portfolio of nonperforming loans made by state-owned banks.

The author also reviews the wider social, political, and economic effects of aging. Probably no other work yet written takes as broad a view of the interaction between development and aging and the government's policy responses as this one. The author notes, for example, that the sharp drop in fertility rates, a process that started well before the introduction of the one-child policy in the early 1980s, has generated serious concern in China that the country's population may begin to shrink rapidly once it has peaked a few decades from now. Few outsiders are aware that these concerns have already led to a relaxation of China's one-child family policy.

This examination of how the private sector—from foreign invested enterprises to thousands of small family businesses in China—has overtaken state-owned industries to become the dominant contributor to China's economic development, and the virtual engine of its job-creating machine, will give both general reader and policy wonk a better handle on the enormous challenges facing China and how they may play out over the coming decades.

Preface

It is difficult to find the right vantage point from which to appreciate the whole picture of an outsized country like China. Its vast lands, teeming population, rich and turbulent history, and varied cultures leave outsiders with much to learn, understand, and comprehend. It is even more difficult to assess the degree of progress China has made in its economic transformation: moving from a poor, stifling, Communist command economy to a major global player with an economy driven by private enterprise. The backdrop for this book—the advent of a period of rapid aging of the population that will redefine China—adds yet one more complicating shift to the big picture of China.

Between 2010 and 2040 the world's most populous nation will enter a period of aging during which the portion of its people 65 and older will rise from approximately 7 percent to somewhere between 25 and 30 percent of its total population. In some cities, the elderly could make up between 33 percent and 50 percent of the population. As China grows old, can it retain the youthful dynamism now driving it?

China will age rapidly because of the one-child policy that began more than a generation ago. Although fertility had already started to decline by the late 1970s, the one-child policy that officially began in 1980 prompted a steady slide in total fertility rates to a level estimated at about 1.5 today. A total fertility rate of 1.5 means that, on average, each woman in China is having 1.5 children during her lifetime, based on the number of births occurring in a given year. By contrast, in the 1970s and earlier, Chinese women routinely had between 5 and 6 children—and more than that in the rural areas where the majority live. Even as China's fertility has collapsed, advances in medical care have led to greatly increased life expectancy. When the People's Republic of China was founded in 1949, life expectancy in China was only 45 for women and 42 for men. Now it is in the 70s and rising. By 2050 life expectancy could be as high as 81 for women and 76 for men. The combination of low fertility and longer life spans will create the phenomenon of an aging China.

This book is an effort to try to capture the broad outlines of the significant economic, market, social, and demographic factors that will shape the future of China and the role that aging will play in the mix of influences. Broad aging of the population is itself a tricky issue because it has never in the past occurred to the degree that it will in the future. Throughout history, nations comprised many younger people and few older people. The traditional population structure is a pyramid with the youngest inhabiting the largest age cohorts at the bottom and the oldest inhabiting the smallest age cohorts at the top. In the future the population pyramid will be turned upside down in some countries, including China. Because no one has lived in a society with more old people than very young people, there is much to learn and understand about how such a society will work differently from societies of the past and present.

The developed world is on the brink of a massive population aging that will lead to population declines in nations such as Japan, Germany, Italy, and Spain. As a consequence, developed nations will face the enormous costs of benefits for the elderly, their economies will grow slowly or decline, and living standards will stagnate. Aging in developed nations has been widely studied and evaluated in academia and by governments.

Less work has been done in assessing the potential impact of aging in developing countries, and efforts in this area represent a venture into only partially charted waters. The impact in China will be occurring against an economic backdrop different from developed countries. The vastness of China and its essentially rural character also make its challenge different from the challenge of the developed countries. Developed nations are aging as wealthy nations with high living standards; but in China, although abject poverty has been significantly reduced, the vast majority of its people are not middle class, as is often the case in developed nations, but working poor.

China's closest neighbors—the newly industrializing economies of South Korea, Taiwan, Hong Kong, and Singapore—are also set to begin their own rapid aging, but first they will have become moderately developed economies. By contrast, China will begin its rapid aging before it has completed its transition to the status of the moderately developed.

While researching this book, I traveled to China and interviewed many people, from ordinary people in the street to key officials in the bureaucracy and informed observers and intellectuals in academia, the government, and the private sector. The generous assistance provided by Chinese authorities has convinced me of their serious and thoughtful commitment to addressing the issues surrounding the impact of aging on China.

As a newcomer to China, I was surprised to find vigorous academic and policy debates in progress about nearly every facet of society, often within the ranks of the government itself and in its think tanks. A great deal of intellectual ferment is taking place. Thinking outside the box about key social, economic, and political issues has received official blessing, and a deep seriousness of purpose guides these efforts. Chinese officials have also sought advice and input from around the globe to help devise and evaluate various designs for benefits for workers and those in need. Of course, this does not mean that all criticism of the government is welcome. Some forms of protest can still result in harsh punishment.

Before China began its opening to the world and its economic transformation, it had a system of very generous benefits provided to urban workers only; rural workers had no such benefits. The old urban benefit system—including generous pensions, health care, housing support, and lifetime job security—has been in retreat as China restructures its mammoth state-owned enterprises. As new businesses are being created, a new benefits system is being assembled piecemeal, creating a patchwork of benefits that varies across the many types of enterprises to be found in China. In the era of reform, Chinese workers have higher incomes but less secure and less generous benefits and sometimes no benefits at all.

For example, employees have a greater responsibility for their own health care while pension benefits have been reduced as a share of one's lifetime income.

My visit to China also helped me understand how difficult it is to implement new policies in a country so decentralized; China has 31 mostly disparate provinces. Although the central government issues edicts and establishes laws for the nation, it is up to provinces, cities, and towns to implement them. Each province goes about implementing policies in its own way and often to suit varying conditions in each province. Implementation of national policies for rural areas can be even more varied in outcome because it is difficult for Beijing to monitor all that occurs in the nation's many villages.

China's economy is further complicated by the kinds of businesses that have evolved. From state-owned enterprises to urban collectives to foreign-invested enterprises, the Chinese economy has a set of players very different from that of any other developing country. When China studies an issue and develops a potential policy to address it, officials try out the new policy on a pilot basis in one area of the country. Even if it is deemed a success in one area, it is quite another proposition to get the policy in place across the entire nation. This has been especially true of new types of employee benefits—including reforms of urban social security and health benefits—to replace those once dominant in the state-owned-enterprise sector. Even so, while much remains to be done, China has made great progress in implementing sweeping reforms of workers' benefits.

The task of evaluating China, its economic progress, and its prospects for dealing with the aging of its population is complicated by the difficulty of getting statistical data that can capture what is going on in China today. Many important sets of data—from the current fertility rate, to the unemployment rate, to the market value of the nation's state-owned enterprises—come with some level of doubt. I have used both official and unofficial data to arrive at a range of measures to capture the state of affairs in such areas as the value of bad loans at China's banks and the deficit in the urban social security system. In some cases, official and unofficial measures of key activities and indicators have been converging toward a common number; when a difference exists, it is often possible to explain why official and unofficial estimates vary.

I reach the end of this long effort of research and writing with a far greater appreciation for China, a country that remains strangely unfamiliar to most outsiders despite decades of opening to the world. I have only scratched the surface of this important subject, and I look forward to the work of others who no doubt will explore this vital topic in more depth.

R.S.E.

Acknowledgments

I would like to thank the China National Working Commission on Aging (CNWCA) for sponsoring my visit to China. I would especially like to thank Xiao Caiwei, director of CNWCA's international department, who helped me plan and conduct my visit, and Yin Wenhui, program director, who set up my interviews and acted as my interpreter. I am also deeply grateful for the assistance provided me by the Institute of Population Studies of the China Academy of Social Sciences and, especially, its director, Cai Fang.

I also am grateful to Pieter Bottelier, former head of the Beijing office of the World Bank, and Stuart H. Leckie, chairman of the Hong Kong Retirement Schemes Association, for reviewing my manuscript and making many helpful suggestions to improve it. In addition, I greatly appreciate the help of Bates Gill, Freeman Chair in China Studies at the Center for Strategic and International Studies (CSIS), and his research assistant, Andrew Thompson, for providing comments to my first draft and helping with key translations.

I would also like to thank John Haley, president and chief executive officer of Watson Wyatt Worldwide, and Sylvester Schieber, director of research at Watson Wyatt, for their help in locating sources in China and their guidance in my research. Watson Wyatt helped set up interviews with private firms in China and with government, academic, and private sources in Hong Kong. I am very thankful for assistance provided by Lisa Huang, who at the time was an intern with Watson Wyatt; she provided countless hours of research and translation assistance and helped locate important sources in China ahead of my visit.

I am grateful for the help provided by Craig Romm, formerly of the Global Aging Initiative at CSIS, in coordinating the research of interns, tracking down sources for this book, and in helping me arrange my travels to China. Finally, I deeply appreciate the research assistance provided by Keisuke Nakashima of the Global Aging Initiative.

1

Introduction and Overview

China is on the brink of a rapid transformation to an aging society that will significantly alter its social structure and shift its relationship with the rest of the world. The transformation is the result of increased longevity and China's one-child policy. In 2000, people aged 65 and over constituted about 7 percent of China's 1.275 billion people.[1] By 2025 those 65 and older will represent 13 percent of China's population of 1.47 billion; and by 2050 they will represent 23 percent of 1.46 billion people, according to the United Nations (UN).[2] A half century from now the masses of China's elderly—332 million strong—will be far greater than the combined elderly populations of North America (United States and Canada), Europe (east and west plus all of Russia), and Japan, whose combined elderly will total 310 million.[3] In 2000, by comparison, China's elderly numbered 87.9 million and represented just over half the combined 168.4 million elderly of North America, Europe, Russia, and Japan (figures 1.1 and 1.2).

China's great demographic transition will add yet another sweeping change to the two other broad transitions under way since 1978: China's transition from a developing to a developed country and its movement from a command to a market economy.[4] The timing of the aging transition makes China's case unique. It will be the first major developing country to become an aging country before it becomes a moderately developed country. By contrast, the Asian "tigers"—South Korea, Taiwan, Singapore, and Hong Kong—all had become moderately developed countries before they began to age rapidly.

Figure 1.1. Population Age 65 and Older, 2000

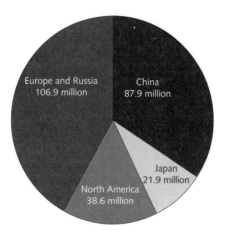

Source: United Nations Population Division, *World Population Ageing 1950-2050* (New York: United Nations, 2002), pp. 78, 96, 178, and 286.

Figure 1.2. Population Age 65 and Older, 2050

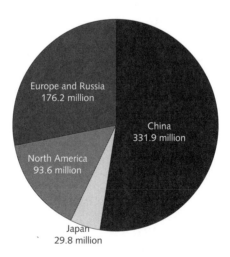

Source: UN Population Division, *World Population Ageing 1950-2050,* pp. 78, 96, 178, and 286.

China's economic transition is itself leading to another demographic transformation: a rural-to-urban migration that is expected to continue steadily over the coming half century. Predictions of just how thoroughly and rapidly China will become an urban country vary widely. The UN projects that the urban portion of China will rise from 27 percent in 2000 to 59.5 percent in 2030.[5] The National Statistics Bureau calculates the level of urbanization in 2000 at 36 percent.[6] Others, such as Cao Gui-Ying, have estimated that urbanization will occur at a slower pace and reach only 39 percent by 2045.[7] International economist Zhang Junlin, director of Asia-Pacific Studies at the China Academy of Social Sciences, calculates that by 2050 China will be 80 percent urban.[8]

Measures of China's future pace of urbanization vary in part because sometimes geographical areas are changed from rural to urban by administrative decision. Many areas identified as villages today are quite large and would likely be defined as urban in many nations. In addition, a fundamental change in family structure has accompanied China's urbanization. Gradually, the traditional Chinese household with several generations living together under one roof is being replaced by the nuclear family—a mother, a father, and, most often, one child—without grandparents or great grandparents.

Children are almost the only source of support for the elderly in the rural areas, where there is no universal social security system in place. As more and more of China's young people migrate to the cities for work, the bonds and ties between them and their rural parents will be stretched and broken. This means that in time more elderly in the rural areas will find themselves without support. Many of those who go to the cities take jobs with enterprises that are either in the informal sector or in the formal sector but that currently do not participate in the social security system. Thus, these young workers are not contributing into a retirement system for their own old age.

As the old command economy dies, so goes with it the elaborate benefit system that was provided through the state-owned enterprises (SOEs). These benefits—part of the "iron rice bowl" set up in the 1950s that provided pensions, health care, housing support, maternity leave, and other benefits—were provided only for the urban population. In time a market economy can be expected to provide a complete system of benefits to replace those that are being lost. Xiaochun Qiao,[9] a professor at Renmin University's Institute of Population Research in Beijing, believes that the pace of China's aging is such that it may be well advanced before the transition to a market economy has provided the new system of benefits that will be needed: "[T]he period of rapid aging will become problematic when the old system has been eliminated, and the new system has not yet been established, or has not yet exerted influence for solving the problems."[10] Qiao suggests that neither the public nor the government is fully aware of the living pressures that will descend on the elderly and the work pressures that will fall on their children. A number of barriers stand in the way of solving these social and economic problems and, he adds, time is short.

Financing legacy pension payments for SOEs will be part of the burden that the central government may have to bear. The urban social security system, which in 2000 covered 106 million of the 212.7 million urban workers in the formal sector,[11] has large unfunded future liabilities, initially officially estimated at about 22.5 percent of gross domestic product (GDP) for 1995.[12] Independent estimates run higher. What these shortfalls suggest is that China will likely need to further reform its social security system to make it more sustainable as well as expand it to include more workers. In time, all non-SOEs will face pressure from workers to provide a host of benefits, including adequate health care coverage for all urban workers and full-time nonagricultural workers in rural areas, as part of China's effort to build a system of benefits in the new market economy.

Economic Reform

China will be better able to bear the growing aging burden if the pace of economic restructuring is given a new boost with economic and legal reforms that allow for more flexibility in restructuring of SOEs. Profitability at SOEs has been flat or declining despite huge efforts at restructuring and, in some cases, massive layoffs. Some firms are bankrupt and have dismal prospects for success.

Further banking reforms and restructuring could allow for a more rational and efficient allocation of an estimated 24.501 trillion yuan[13] ($2.960 trillion) deposited at financial institutions by businesses, organizations, and households. Funds in China's command economy were traditionally allocated by government leaders to SOEs. Since the reform era began in 1978, growing and dynamic non-SOEs have often been starved for capital. Despite reforms, funds available at banks continue to flow primarily to inefficient and sometimes bankrupt SOEs although efforts have been under way to make funds available to viable private business firms to borrow from the state-owned banks.

In 1984, the central government shifted responsibility for providing capital to SOEs from the state budget to the state-owned commercial banks. The banks, in fulfilling this role, began to accumulate a growing portfolio of nonperforming loans. Beijing acknowledged the problem in 1999 when it began to set up asset management companies (AMCs) to take over many of the nonperforming loans in order to improve the balance sheets at the banks. Yet the banks continue to make bad loans.

Provided it addresses adequately the pressing reforms needed to further the restructuring of its SOEs and its banking system, China is expected to be able to continue the rapid gains it has made since 1978 in per capita income. Per capita GDP has zoomed in China from $267 (417 yuan) per year in 1980[14] to $1,090 in 2003.[15] Future gains will rest on continued investment in improving productivity and continued high economic growth rates. If the expected benefits materialize, children in the future will enjoy a higher living standard when they become adults and will thus be better able to support their elderly parents. The government, too, will be better able to afford the benefits needed by those who will be left without support and pay costs associated with bad debts at banks and the shortfall in the social security system.

Beyond the problems facing the banking sector, China also needs to address problems in its financial sector. Its markets are immature and plagued by legal and illegal stock manipulation and speculation. The markets are short on major institutional market players with the long-term risk-management and investing skills needed to strengthen and stabilize the markets. The market is so thin that enterprises rely almost entirely on bank lending and not the issuance of equity to raise capital. The government treasury bond market is also uneven, with little investor interest in long-term bonds.

Institutional investors could become a positive force for deepening and strengthening the country's financial markets if China succeeds in advancing pension reform that provides real funding in the individual accounts created in 1995. Investment choices for funds that actually accrue in individual accounts are now made not by individuals but by local social security bureaus on behalf of funds pooled from many enterprises, sometimes at the local township level and sometimes at the provincial level. To the extent that China develops a prefunded pension system, functioning markets can help provide the returns needed to reduce the burden on current workers; this in turn could help raise living standards.

Job Growth

Since the 1997–1998 Asian economic crises, the pace of economic restructuring has slowed in both the rural and urban areas, according an analysis by the Organization for Economic Cooperation and Development (OECD).[16] As a result, more broad systemic reforms are needed to address the problems that have emerged from China's incomplete transition to a market economy, the study contends. Data on employment in the state sector and growth of the private sector suggest, however, that restructuring has not slowed but has continued at a steady place.

The central government has every reason to encourage growth of the private sector because this is where jobs are being created while the state-owned sector is losing jobs. The central government is anxious to promote policies that help ensure that the economy grows at a sufficient pace, 7 percent, to keep unemployment below 7 percent. Unemployment rates above that level are seen as potentially leading to widespread social unrest. Social instability could ultimately be more damaging for a smooth economic transition than some of the other problematic policies that the central government has pursued or allowed. In recent years, in fact, the economy has grown at rates somewhat higher than 7 percent, but it has not been enough to reduce unemployment rates.

To maintain a high rate of growth, China will need to make more of an effort to see that banks allocate credit on a level playing field to state-owned, non-state-owned, and, especially, private enterprises. China will also need to find ways to reduce regional protectionism that puts domestic investment at a disadvantage vis-à-vis foreign direct investment (FDI). China has been extraordinarily successful in attracting FDI, becoming its number-one recipient in 2002, but it can do even better. To attract more significant levels of FDI with significant advances in technology transfer, China will have to create a regime that allows foreign investors in China to earn a reasonable return and repatriate their gains. Finally, China must avoid overinvestment in redundant capacity—China's automobile manufacturing industry currently suffers from this—which often takes place at the local level as part of local policies aimed at economic development and job creation.

Unemployment, then, is a key indicator to watch; however, it is not always clear what the true unemployment level is. Officially, there are two categories of unemployed workers—those classified as unemployed and those classified as laid off. In September 2003, the number of unemployed was 7.93 million or 4.3 percent of the labor force, and the number of laid-off workers was 3.1 million. The combined unemployed number was 11.03 million or 6.0 percent of China's estimated 184.7 million urban workers in the formal sector who are not self-employed. That total represents a decline in the portion of the workforce unemployed compared with one year earlier: in September 2002, 7.52 million were officially unemployed and 4.94 million were officially laid off; this was 6.2 percent China's estimated 192.8 million urban workers in the formal sector who were not self-employed.[17]

A number of economists outside of government have suggested that the real unemployment rate is probably closer to 7 or 8 percent in the formal sector. Unemployment has generated significant levels of labor unrest. Layoffs in such places as Daqing, Liaoyang, and Chongqing have sparked huge protests. Smaller protests are becoming quite common.

China, eager to maintain peace in the labor force, has pursued policies it believes will keep unemployment levels from rising precipitously. Official unemployment statistics are likely to jump after 2004, however, when the government phases out programs for an estimated 3.1 million laid-off workers; workers who will not yet have found employment will be reclassified as unemployed. A number of factors will add to the ranks of the unemployed, said Minister of Labor and Social Security Zhen Silin when he announced a new round of policies aimed at accelerating economic growth to create more new jobs. The country will face a rising oversupply of labor because the number of new job seekers entering the market is expected to average 15 million a year between 2004 and 2020. The economy must grow at least 7 percent to create 8 million jobs per year, Zhen stated.

In addition, the ranks of redundant and unemployed will swell as more unprofitable SOEs continue to close down during economic restructuring. Economic growth, while a necessary factor in boosting employment numbers, is not as powerful a job growth engine as it was in the past. During the 1980s, a 1 percent increase in GDP led to 2.4 million new jobs; during the 1990s, however, each percentage point of economic growth resulted in only 700,000 new jobs.[18]

Rapid economic growth in the coming years can also better prepare China for another social burden that lies ahead in the 2020s, a decade when the costs of benefits due to the elderly will rise sharply. To the extent China will have made the transition to a moderately developed market economy by then, it will be in a better position to assume the burden of increased benefits to the elderly. China must address the level of the need now in its reforms of the social security, social welfare, and health care systems and be prepared for a much bigger social burden for long-term care of the elderly, who will have no one to turn to in their hour of need.

Global Role

China's full transition to a market economy, with appropriate and reliable legal and regulatory mechanisms and viable markets and financial institutions, will give the nation an opportunity to play a major role on the world economic stage. A prospering, stable, growing China may be able to address imbalances in the world economy that occur because of the impact of aging in developed countries.

In North America, Europe, and Japan, a surge in the number of elderly will put severe strains on the budgets of these governments as they struggle to sustain benefits. Debt burdens will rise and the pace of economic growth will slow. Based on current fertility rates in such countries as Japan, Germany, and Italy, economies will decline as populations decline. As savings rates decline in the developed countries, the pool of savings in China—which currently has a savings rate estimated as high as 40 percent—may help provide some of the funds needed for investment both inside and outside China and for borrowing by governments around the world. China's markets may also offer Western and Japanese pension fund managers opportunities to earn returns higher than they might earn from investing at home. In addition, China's large labor pool can be a good match with investment capital from developed countries.

China's investors may also play a positive global role after 2025. Beginning then, the value of equities in markets with today's highest level of pension assets—the United States, the United Kingdom, Japan, the Netherlands, Switzerland, and Canada—will be under pressure and may possibly stagnate or decline.[19] In this environment, China's institutional investors—provided they have the right to invest in overseas assets—can diversify their risks by acquiring developed-world equity assets. To the extent that China's future institutional investors have accumulated a large and growing asset base, their overseas investments could offset some of the decline in demand by investors in the West. The Chinese demand for developing-world equities, however, is unlikely to exceed the decline in demand in developed countries unless those countries have also developed newly funded retirement schemes that would increase the demand for their own domestic equities.

China's further economic development and integration of its economy and markets into the global economy will make it more interdependent with the rest of the world. This should, in time, be further reflected in its foreign policy. China's economic gains during the 1990s, for example, have transformed its views of itself and the world, according to Zhang Yunling and Tang Shiping.[20] A more confident China has emerged as the country's economic growth has given it greater stature and influence in world affairs, the authors claim. As a result, China is less likely to overreact to changes on the international scene, including its dealings with the United States and the shift of Russia from a Eurasian to an Atlantic identity under Vladimir Putin. Zhang and Tang believe that China rightly does not see this as a threat; instead, China is likely to be more proactive in protecting its interests without picking fights. On the other hand, a rising China will alter the shape of geopolitics in East and Southeast Asia. Thus, the potential for tension and conflict with neighbors and the United States will remain.

Finally, all the potentially positive developments that could help China deal with the challenge of its aging population could be diminished without further governance reform to accompany the economic reform. The stability of China's political system has been strengthened over the years—a fact demonstrated by its smooth transitions to a new party leader in November 2002 and a new government in March 2003. The once-closed system has evolved enough to increasingly provide an officially sanctioned means of criticism, dialogue, and innovation. Yet the pace of innovation in governance seems to have stalled. Indeed, the lagging evolution of China's political system compared with the rapidity of its transition to a market economy may be partly blamed for China's enduring and widespread corruption.[21]

The political leaders of the fourth generation of Communist rule headed by General Secretary Hu Jintao have recently taken steps that indicate they will pay more heed to a rising number of calls for political and governance reform from key respected scholars and Communist Party theoreticians such as economist Hu Angang[22] and political scientist He Zengke.[23] These scholars identify corruption as the most pressing problem of Chinese society, a problem they say has proliferated as a result of opportunities for enrichment that have resulted from the country's transition to a market economy without a suitable transition in governance.

Notes

1. United Nations Population Division, *World Population Ageing 1950–2050* (New York: United Nations, 2002), p. 178.

2. Ibid.

3. Ibid., pp. 78, 96, 178, and 286. Out of China's 1.462 billion people, 22.7 percent (331.9 million), will be 65 and older. Out of North America's population of 603.3 million for the United States and Canada, 21.4 percent (93.6 million) will be 65 and older. Out of Europe and Russia's combined 603.3 million population, 29.2 percent (176.2 million) will be 65 and older. Out of Japan's 109.2 million population, 36.4 percent (39.8 million) will be 65 and older.

4. Athar Hussain, "Social Welfare in China in the Context of Three Transitions," Working paper no. 66 (Palo Alto, Calif.: Stanford University, Center for Research on Economic Development and Policy Reform, August 2000), http://credpr.stanford.edu/pdf/credpr66.pdf.

5. United Nations Population Division, *World Urbanization Prospects: The 2001 Revision* (New York: United Nations, 2002), table A.2., p. 165.

6. Urban population of 458.4 million and rural population of 807.4 million in 2000, from *China Statistical Yearbook 2002* (Beijing: National Bureau of Statistics of China, China Statistics Press, 2002), table 4.4.

7. Cao Gui-Ying, "The Future Population of China: Prospects to 2045 by Place of Residence and by Level of Education" (National University of Singapore, Asian MetaCentre for Population and Sustainable Development Analysis, April 20, 2000, mimeo.).

8. Cable News Network, "China at 2050," 1999, http://asia.cnn.com/SPECIALS/china.50/50.beyond/china.at.2050 (accessed 1999).

9. The family name is Qiao, which in China is normally placed first, ahead of the given name; however, some Chinese reverse the order, as Xiaochun Qiao has done.

10. Xiaochun Qiao, "From Decline of Fertility to Transition of Age Structure: Ageing and Its Policy Implications in China," *Genus* 17, no. 1 (January–March 2001): 57–81.

11. Data from China's MLSS cited on table 1, p. 5, of Song Xiaowu, "China's Social Security System and Old-Age Pension Funds" (paper presented at the Asian Development Bank Annual Meeting, Shanghai, May 8–12, 2002).

12. Kong Jingyuan, "Implicit Pension Debt and Its Repayment," in *Restructuring China's Social Security System*, ed. Wang Megkui, China Development Research Foundation Series (Beijing: Foreign Languages Press, 2002), pp. 175–176. Project to calculate the implicit debt was overseen by He Ping, deputy director of the Social Insurance Institute of the MLSS. The calculation for the implicit debt for 1995 was 1,317.428 billion yuan ($150 billion at the exchange rate of 8.27815 on October 2002), representing 22.5 percent of 1995's GDP of 5,847.81 billion yuan ($706 billion at the exchange rate of 8.27815 on October 2002).

13. Data for August 2004 from People's Bank of China, http://www.pbc.gov.cn/english/diaochatongji/tongjishuju/gofile.asp?file=2004S1.htm. Currency conversion: 24.501 trillion yuan renminbi or $2.169 trillion at exchange rate of 0.120821 on October 16, 2003. Dollars refer to U.S. dollars.

14. *China Statistical Yearbook 2003* (Beijing: National Bureau of Statistics of China, China Statistics Press, 2003), p. 55. 417 yuan equals $267 at the 1979 exchange rate of 1.56.

15. Xinhua News Agency, "9.1% Surge Epitomizes Sound Growth of Economy," January 20, 2004, http://news.xinhuanet.com/english/2004-01/20/content_1285767.htm.

16. Organization for Economic Cooperation and Development (OECD), *China in the World Economy* (Paris: OECD, 2002).

17. Ministry of Labor and Social Security, http://www.molss.gov.cn.

18. "Jobless Situation to Stay Grave for Years," *China Daily*, November 6, 2003, p. 1.

19. Robert Stowe England, *Global Aging and Financial Markets: Hard Landings Ahead?* (Washington, D.C.: Center for Strategic and International Studies, 2002).

20. Zhang Yunling and Tang Shiping, "More Self-Confident China Will Be a Responsible Power," *Straits Times*, October 2, 2002.

21. He Zengke, "Fighting Corruption through Institutional Innovations toward Good Governance" (Beijing: China Center for Comparative Politics and Economics, 2000).

22. Hu Angang is a professor of economics at Qinghua University and director of the Center for China Studies at the Chinese Academy of Social Sciences.

23. He Zengke is a political scientist at the Center for Comparative Politics and Economics in Beijing.

2

Demography Shapes the Society

Demography is destiny. While variables may mute demography's impact, significant demographic change is a very powerful force that can reshape society. The broad outline of how demographic change will affect China during the next 50 years can be predicted with some degree of certainty. To the extent that policymakers understand the shape of those changes, they will have the opportunity to take steps to be better prepared to face the resulting challenges.

Demographic change comprises longevity and mortality, fertility, and immigration. In China, the impact of immigration will likely be nil because China is not open to immigration. Inside China, however, during the next 50 years, economic change will drive a great wave of human migration from rural to urban areas. This migration, along with a progressive reclassification of some rural areas as urban, will transform China from an overwhelmingly rural society to one that is mostly urban (see pages 28–30 for further discussion). The rapid pace of China's economic development will drive the pace of this change.

Demographer Xiaochun Qiao has forecast that China's working-age population (ages 15 to 64) will grow from 861 million in 2000 to 1.006 billion in 2025.[1] However, the pace of growth of the workforce will slow dramatically in the years following 2010, after the total working-age population reaches 975 million. After 2025, the size of the working-age population will decline to 908 million in 2050.[2]

Longevity

Longevity in China has made remarkable gains. By 1995 the life expectancy at birth for women had reached 71.78 years while it was 68.13 for men.[3] This represents an enormous and steady gain over the life expectancy numbers for 1949 at the establishment of the People's Republic of China. In 1949 the life expectancy for women was 44.8 and for men it was 42.3.[4] Future gains are likely to bring China closer to longevity levels in the developed world.

Xiaochun Qiao projects China's population and age distribution out to 2050; he assumes that fertility will rise slightly owing to a relaxation of the one-child policy and that life expectancy at birth will rise to 81.0 years for women and 76.4 years for men. He finds that China's median age, which he estimates to be 30.8 on the basis of data in the 2000 census,[5] will be 40 in 2030[6]—double the median age of 20 back in 1964, a transformation that will have occurred over a period of only 66 years. Qiao expects a population peak for all of China sometime between 2030 and 2035—earlier than official projections—with the numbers of elderly increasing at about 3 percent a year now. Qiao calls the current 3 percent rate the "speeding-up period"; after today's speeding-up period, from 2010 to 2040, the rate of increase of the elderly will enter a long "high-speed period."

During China's high-speed aging, the speed will vary. During the first five years after 2010, the size of the over-65 population will grow at 5.1 percent annually. The fast pace will then slow to nearly half that level—but still very rapid—after 2015. Then it will resume at its high speed—above 4 percent and sometimes close to 5 percent—for the next 10 years. After 2030, the pace of aging will decelerate rapidly, falling to 0.3 percent around 2040. Qiao calls the time from 2040 to 2050 the "speed-down period," as the size of the elderly population approaches a new equilibrium compared with the size of the working-age population. The irregular pattern of China's gains in its elderly population can be seen in figure 2.1. This rapid aging process will drive up the number of Chinese age 65 and over from 88.26 million in the 2000 census[7] to 108 million in 2010, 159 million in 2020, 221 million in 2030, and 300 million in 2045 (figure 2.2 and table 2.1).

Figure 2.1. Five-Year Increase Rate for Total and Elderly Population, 1990–2050

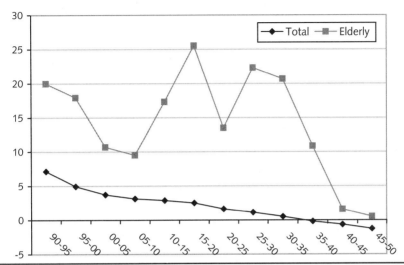

Source: Xiaochun Qiao, "From Decline of Fertility to Transition of Age Structure: Aging and Its Policy Implications in China," *Genus* 17, no. 1 (January–March 2001), p. 65.

Figure 2.2. China's Changing Age Structure, 2000–2050

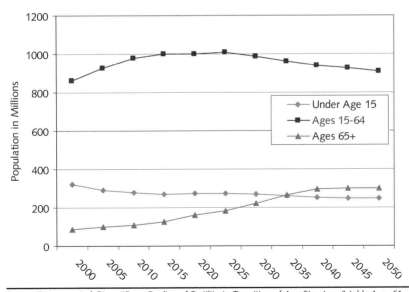

Source: Data reported Qiao, "From Decline of Fertility to Transition of Age Structure," table 1, p. 61.

Table 2.1. Age Structure of China's Population, 1953–2050

Year	Total Population (millions)	Number (millions)			Proportion (percentage)			Median
		0–14	15–64	65+	0–14	15–64	65+	
1953	567.45	205.48	336.57	25.04	36.38	59.31	4.41	22.8
1964	694.58	280.67	384.45	24.58	40.70	55.74	3.56	20.4
1982	1003.91	337.25	617.39	49.27	33.59	61.50	4.91	22.7
1990	1130.51	313.00	754.52	62.99	27.70	66.72	5.58	25.3
1995	1207.78	321.66	813.98	75.27	26.56	67.20	6.24	27.7
2000	1271.15	320.72	861.30	89.13	25.23	67.76	7.01	30.1
2005	1318.58	293.39	926.53	98.66	22.25	70.27	7.48	32.3
2010	1360.28	277.13	975.12	108.04	20.37	71.69	7.94	34.2
2015	1399.61	271.44	1001.40	126.77	19.39	71.55	9.06	35.6
2020	1435.03	273.84	1002.04	159.15	19.08	69.83	11.09	36.8
2025	1462.67	275.19	1006.83	180.65	18.81	68.84	12.35	38.3
2030	1479.39	269.77	988.67	220.96	18.24	66.83	14.94	40.0
2035	1487.28	269.77	960.41	266.67	17.50	64.57	17.93	41.2
2040	1484.78	252.14	937.07	295.57	16.98	63.11	19.91	42.1
2045	1475.17	248.31	926.59	300.28	16.83	62.81	20.36	42.4
2050	1456.47	246.48	908.08	301.83	16.92	62.35	20.72	42.4

Sources: Qiao, "From Decline of Fertility to Transition of Age Structure," p. 61. Data for 1953, 1964, 1982, and 1990 are calculated from relevant population censuses; 1995 data are from the adjustment of 1995 National One Percent Population Survey; data after 2000 are calculated, based on results of population projection.

Note: Population figures for 1953, 1964, 1982, and 1990 did not include the indirect estimated population, unknown age population, and military population.

Figure 2.3. Elderly Dependency Ratio, 2000–2050

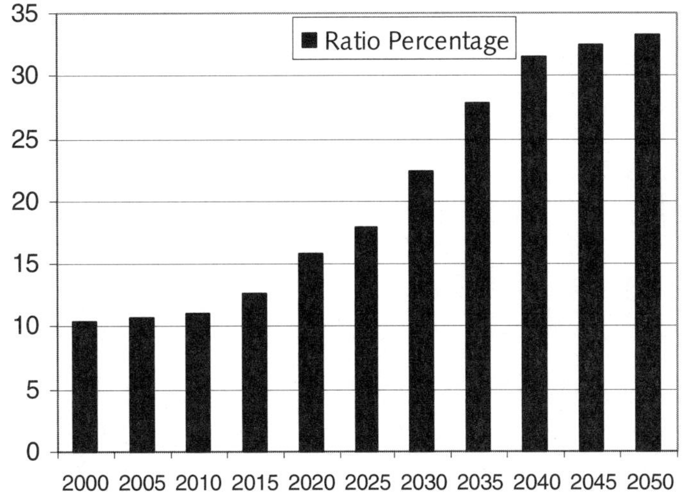

Source: Data reported in Qiao, "From Decline of Fertility to Transition of Age Structure, " chart 4, p. 66.

The Elderly Dependency Ratio

The key ratio for measuring the impact of aging is the elderly dependency ratio: the number of elderly as a percentage of the number of people of working age (ages 15 to 64). Unlike most developed countries—where the working-age populations are expected to decline after 2010—China's working-age population will continue to rise until 2025.

Those aged 65 and over will rise from 7 percent of the population in 2000 to just under 8 percent in 2010, according to Qiao.[8] In 2015, the elderly will be 9 percent of the population; in 2020, 11 percent; in 2030, 15 percent; and in 2040, 20 percent.[9] After 2040 the percentage of elderly will stabilize in the low 20s.

The elderly dependency ratio will chart a similar path, rising from 10.30 percent in 2000 to 12.66 percent in 2015 (figure 2.3). When the elderly dependency ratio is 10.30 percent, it means that 100 working-age adults will support 10.30 people aged 65 and over. After 2015, the dependency ratio will begin to soar rapidly, rising to 15.88 percent in 2020, 17.94 percent in 2025, and 22.35 percent in 2030. After 2030, the pace of the rise in the dependency ratio will slow sharply, rising gradually to 33.23 percent in 2050 (table 2.2).

Table 2.2. Five-Year Increases of the Indexes of the Elderly Population

Year	Total Population (percentage)	Elderly at Age 65+ (percentage)	Proportion of Population at Age 65+	Increase in Percentage Points of Proportion of Elderly	Dependent Ratio for the Elderly, Age 65+ (percentage)	Increase in Percentage of Proportion of Dependent Ratio
1990	7.14	19.98	5.58	0.67	8.33	0.95
1995	4.95	17.94	6.24	0.77	9.28	1.07
2000	3.73	10.69	7.01	0.47	10.35	0.30
2005	3.16	9.51	7.48	0.46	10.65	0.43
2010	2.89	17.34	7.94	1.12	11.08	1.58
2015	2.53	25.54	9.06	2.03	12.66	3.22
2020	1.63	13.51	11.09	1.26	15.88	2.06
2025	1.14	22.31	12.35	2.59	17.94	4.41
2030	0.53	20.68	14.94	2.99	22.35	5.42
2035	-0.17	10.84	17.93	1.98	27.77	3.77
2040	-0.65	1.59	19.91	0.45	31.54	0.87
2045	-1.27	0.52	20.36	0.36	32.41	0.82
2050			20.72		33.23	

Source: Qiao, "From Decline of Fertility to Transition of Age Structure," p. 66; also, *China Statistics Yearbook 2001* and *Statistics of the Ministry of Labor and Social Security.*

The Impact of a Rising Elderly Dependency Ratio

Data show that the burden of taking care of the elderly, while rising steadily until 2020, begins to soar after that until it reaches a plateau in 2040. The burden of care for the elderly will fall on families in rural areas and in urban areas where the elderly have no social security or pension. The central and provincial governments are likely to have to shoulder the burden of sustaining the urban social security system, as well as providing a safety net for those elderly who are not covered. The elderly will face a difficult time in obtaining health care, as fewer and fewer of the workforce will be retiring with the kind of retiree health care protection that workers had from SOEs. Those SOEs that have retained some protections for retirees will face pressures to reduce or eliminate this coverage.

Fertility

China's change in fertility rates has taken an erratic course as fertility has fallen from very high levels in 1949 to very low levels at the beginning of the twenty-first century. Fertility is measured as both a crude birthrate (the number of births per 1,000 people) and the total fertility rate (TFR, the number of children that would be born to each woman if she were to live to the end of her childbearing years and bear children at each age in accordance with prevailing age-specific fertility rates). In China the total fertility rate has fallen from 6.4 in 1949 to a level well below 2.0 in 2000, a historic change that over the next 50 years will turn China's population pyramid upside down. Demographers differ on what an accurate measure of China's TFR might be. China's 2000 census, for example, reported a very low TFR of 1.22[10]—"a number no one in China believes and no one uses," according to Xiaochun Qiao,[11] who previously worked at the Department of Population, Statistical Bureau, and the Census Office of Liaoning Province.

One-Child Policy

China's family policy evolved in line with official concerns by the central government about the ability of China to feed its enormous population. In the early 1970s—a time when the fear of overpopulation was a popular global theme—China began to encourage couples to restrict the number of children to only two. In 1980, it officially began the one-child policy, but it was not defined in law until December 2001.

This policy was adopted more quickly in the cities than in the rural areas, where families with a female baby could have a second child with the hope of having a male. (Couples could also have a second child if the first child was disabled, or after a divorce and remarriage, among other exceptions.)

The government sometimes uses draconian measures to enforce the one-child policy. Violators have been fired from their jobs and denied social benefits or have had to pay huge fines. Some women have undergone forced abortions and sterilizations.[12] Although officials long denied these abuses had occurred, in 1998, State Family Planning Commission minister Zhang Weiqing conceded that "cases of forced abortion and sterilization occur from time to time, especially in rural areas, in spite of strict government prohibition."[13]

With birthrates falling well below replacement rate in the 1990s and early 2000s, the government moved in 2001 to liberalize and codify its one-child policy in China's first family-planning law.[14] The intent of the law, officials said, was to make the one-child policy more transparent, humanitarian, and flexible. The law allows local authorities considerable discretion in creating exceptions to the one-child policy and in deciding how to enforce it. For example, the law provides that rural residents can have a second child if the first is a girl. The law prohibits the use of ultrasound technology to determine the gender of the unborn child and bans abortion based on gender preferences. Regardless, ultrasound continues to be used to determine the gender of the unborn child and leads to abortions of unwanted female children.

The family planning law went into force in September 2002. Anhui Province was reportedly among the first to take advantage of the new law by allowing some couples to have two children, including coal miners and divorced couples who had only one child in their previous marriages.[15] In contrast, Guangdong raised the financial penalty for additional children from twice to eight times the yearly salary of couples.[16] In 2001, the city of Guangzhou, the capital of Guangdong Province, had 10,229 births that were second children, 16 percent of the total births for that year.[17] Another 1,059 births occurred where couples already had at least two children.[18] Families continue to defy the one-child policy, as fertility data reveal. Sometimes people pay a hefty financial penalty to government officials for having additional children in hopes of having a male child—a practice popularly known as "buying a son."

Demographic Effects of the One-Child Policy

Chinese officials report they have prevented 330 million births since the beginning of the one-child policy,[19] meaning that today China's population would be 1.6 billion instead of the current 1.275 billion. The China Family Planning Association continues to maintain its goal of limiting China's total population peak to 1.6 billion by 2050. Recent declines in fertility suggest that China's population peak will fall as much as 100 million below the limit targeted by officials.

China's annual data that contain crude birthrates are taken from surveys of 1.3 million people. Because of China's one-child policy, launched in 1980, households in which a second, third, or additional birth took place are unlikely to report that fact because of possible severe penalties for violating the one-child policy. Demographers can reliably say that there is underreporting of additional children because later censuses and surveys reveal a larger population of children at each age than was reported in the crude birthrates collected in annual surveys for the years they would have been born.

Officials have not released an official TFR rate since fertility rates fell below 2.0 in 1992. Demographers, however, have taken crude birthrates, which are released annually and converted them into a TFR rate. The most recently released crude birthrate is 12.86 for 2002 (figure 2.4).[20] If relationships between the crude birthrate and TFR found in the 1990 census are used, the 2002 TFR would be 1.39. Stuart H. Leckie, an actuary and chairman of the Hong Kong Retirement Schemes Association, estimates China's TFR at 1.6.[21] Even if China's TFR is as low as 1.6 or 1.5 in a given year, that should be seen as a snapshot of changing birthrates within China and will need to be repeated in later years to verify the trend, cautions Athar Hussain.[22]

Figure 2.4. Crude Birth Rate, 1978–2002

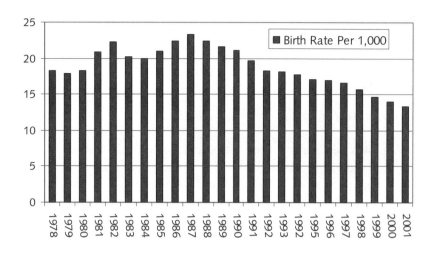

Source: *China Statistical Yearbook 2003*, table 4.2.

If China's real fertility rate is as low as 1.5 and remains at this level or lower, its impact on Chinese society will be felt only gradually—at first slowing Chinese population gains over the next decades before accelerating the decline after China's population reaches its peak. Authorities at the State Family Planning Commission of China expect the nation's population to peak in 2045 at 1.534 billion people.[23] The population is expected to remain at that level afterward. This projection assumes that China's fertility rate will rise to and remain at or near 2.1, the level needed for a population to continuously replace itself (assuming a constant mortality rate).

The State Family Planning Commission also projects that China's working-age population (ages 15 to 60) will grow from 828 million in 2000[24] to 1.013 billion in 2025, with an annual growth rate of 0.84 percent.[25] China's working-age population will decline after that, falling to 898 million in 2070 before recovering to around 900 to 920 million; it is expected to stabilize at this level, according to official projections.[26]

The aging of China's population is already rapid and is expected to accelerate for a long time before it slows and stabilizes.

The China Population Information and Research Center reports that the portion of China's population that is elderly will increase at a pace equal to 0.1 percent each year until 2010.[27] After 2010 the pace will greatly accelerate, to a rate of 0.4 percent each year, and continue at that fast pace until 2040.[28] From 2040 to 2060 the pace will slow to 0.1 percent each year. In the years after 2060 the proportion and number of elderly will remain stable along with the total overall population, the information center estimates.[29]

A sharper picture of the pace of growth of the elderly population can be seen by measuring the rate of growth of elderly each year as a percentage of the current elderly population. The population 60 years of age and older, for example, has been growing for several years by 3 percent per year while the population over 80 is growing at 5 percent per year, according to a March 2001 report by Zhu Zhixin, director of the National Bureau of Statistics and head of the leading group for the National Census of the State Council.[30] China, therefore, is annually adding 3.8 million more elderly over 60 and 500,000 more elderly over 80 years of age.[31] Because retirement age in China is lower than in most developed countries—60 for men, 50 for factory women, and 55 for white-collar women—one also has to look at the size of the population over 60 (not only the population over 65) to get an idea of the level of burden that aging will impose on the country. Zhu projects that, by 2040, 400 million Chinese will be age 60 and over (26 percent of the population).

The potential burden for society, then, will be larger than suggested by UN numbers—23 percent of the population age 65 and over in 2050. In the future, China's cities will be enclaves of the oldest people. Zhu predicts that by 2050 between 33 percent and 50 percent of the population of some cities will be age 60 or older.[32] There could, however, be considerable variety in the age profiles of cities. Some cities, like Shenzhen, could grow younger because of immigration of young people.

Yet, these potentially large societal burdens may be bigger than Zhu predicts. If China's TFR is 1.5 and remains at this level indefinitely, the patterns of total population, working-age population, and elderly population described by Chinese officials will differ. Population totals and working-age totals will not stabilize at fairly high levels and will, instead, enter a prolonged decline. China's aging pattern after 2040 could resemble the outlook for

Japan, Germany, Italy, and Spain—all of which are expected to have significant and continuing population declines during the twenty-first century—with their very low fertility rates that range from 1.1 to 1.4.

While the aging of China will accelerate between 2010 and 2040, the pace of aging will not be a steadily upward-sloping line. It will instead be an uneven line reflecting the dramatic swings in birthrates during China's baby boom from the early 1950s to the early 1970s. During the 1950s, China's fertility and birthrates were very high during most years; TFR ranged from 5.7 to 6.5 per woman, continuing a high fertility pattern going back decades. Then China was plunged into the chaotic Great Leap Forward from 1958 to 1961 and suffered a famine that led to the deaths of as many as 30 million people,[33] more people than China lost during the World War II years from 1937 to 1945. During the Great Leap Forward, birthrates plummeted and TFR was nearly halved from 6.4 in 1957 to 3.3 in 1961. Death rates rose sharply, leading to an extremely rare population decline of 4.5 million in 1960.[34] At the time, the population had been increasing by approximately 20 to 24 million a year. Following this temporary demographic shift, China resumed its baby boom from 1962 to 1971. In 1972, TFR fell below 5 and started trending downward, falling below 3 in 1977. Fertility remained well above replacement rates from 1978 to 1981 but fell steadily during the 1980s, especially after the official announcement of the one-child policy in 1980.

Gender Imbalance Caused by the One-Child Policy

China is now trying to address a new problem born of its one-child policy and the persistent desire of families to have a male child who is expected to take care of his parents in their old age. This desire to make sure that the one and only child is a male child has led to abortions of unborn females and a rise in the ratio of male to female births. Chinese couples have been able to detect the gender of an unborn child with portable ultrasound scanners that have spread throughout the countryside, especially in the southern and eastern provinces. The procedure is available in most small-town hospitals. Even though it has been outlawed, its use continues to spread. In 2000, the gender imbalance reached 116 males to 100 females,[35] up sharply from the 1990 census, when the imbalance was 111 to 100.[36] In some areas the gender imbalance is significantly higher than 116:100. The worldwide gender birth imbalance, which occurs naturally when there is no medical intervention, is 105 to 100. If one looks at the gender imbalance more closely in the raw data of the 2000 census, one can see the desperation by parents as they have additional children after the first one or two are females. The gender ratio is 107:100 for the first child, but it is 152:100 for the second child and 160:100 for the third child.[37]

As generations with unbalanced ratios of male to female come of age, the impact on Chinese society is likely to be disruptive and harmful. The breakdown of the Communists' strict moral code has allowed prostitution and the sex industry to flourish in China. The growth of the sex industry is a leading cause of the rapid spread of AIDS. Premarital sex, once rare, is said to be predominant. In addition, the sex industry is thriving partly because of the movement of as many as 130 million people from rural to urban areas, with tens of million more expected in the coming years. These uprooted young men and women are more likely to become involved in sexual activity that can spread AIDS.

Chinese officials are increasingly expressing worries publicly about the social impact of the gender imbalance. In September 2002, Tian Xueyuan, vice chairman of the semiofficial China Population Society, was quoted by the Communist Party's *Outlook* magazine: "Gender imbalance will breed many moral and social problems if we can't correct or effectively check it in time," Tian said. "The risk of instability for families and the public will rise."[38] The excess of men could also create more competition for some jobs in 10 to 20 years, he added.

An excess of tens of millions of single men also prompts national security concerns. A study of the potential impact of the future gender imbalance by Valerie Hudson and Andrea Den Boer[39] concludes that in 20 years the imbalance could threaten China's stability and endanger its prospects for greater political freedom.[40] They project that by 2020 China will have 29 million to 33 million surplus males between the ages of 15 and 34. The researchers note that the presence of such large numbers of unmarried men has shaken China before, for example, the Nian Rebellion in Shandong Province in the mid-1800s when in Shandong there were 129 men for every 100 women and approximately one-quarter of the men never married. Some of the bachelors turned to banditry and later to rebellion against the Qing dynasty. During the peak of their influence, 100,000 Nian rebels gained control over 6 million people. The government battled them for 17 years before the revolt was completely suppress. Hudson and Den Boer suggest that the surplus males in China are likely to be from the lowest strata of society and be highly represented in China's floating migrant population.

China's efforts to make its one-child policy more flexible seem to be aimed partly at reducing the gender birth imbalance and, indirectly, at easing the worries parents have about their caregivers in their old age.

One-Child Policy Affects Care of Elderly

Qiao contends that the one-child policy has dealt China a demographic hand that officials and ordinary people will find difficult to play. China will age so fast that aging will outpace changes in the social economy and the institutions and conventions of Chinese society: "The impact will be profound and the conflicts between them will be inevitable and incredible."[41] In 1994[42] and 1995,[43] Lin Jiang created simulations of the impact of aging on family structure and found that the burden of supporting elderly parents is likely to increase enormously, but the relative increase in that burden will differ in urban and rural areas.

Urban areas. Because of differences in birthrates in urban and rural areas since the beginning of the one-child policy, the old-age burden will quadruple for urban families, but it will only double for rural families by 2030. Lin's studies suggest that the family alone will not be able to bear this burden, and Lin recommends public assistance, particularly to rural families, to prevent families from being unduly burdened. Lin also recommends having the younger elderly help take care of the older elderly, which has become increasingly possible because of the improved health of China's older citizens.

Qiao also simulates the potential burden on families.[44] Using data on the number of women born at different times and data on the number of children by each age group born to them, Qiao calculates how the burden will be distributed across Chinese society. For his simulation, he assumed that no children will die before their mothers reach age 65 (meaning that the average number of children living in 1990 will not change), that all mothers will be alive to age 65, and that women age 30 and over will have no additional children.

Qiao found that urban women who were age 45 to 49 in 1990, for example, had an average of 3.03 children alive at that time. These women, who turn 65 between 2006 and 2010, have good prospects for finding support from their children. Town women from the same age group had 3.35 children alive in 1990, giving them more family support than the city women can count on. Finally, rural women in this group had 3.69 children alive in 1990. Thus, they have the most family support resources.

Qiao also found the outlook for younger women less promising. Urban women who were aged 30 to 34 in 1990 (in their 40s in the mid-2000s), had an average of 1.30 children alive in 1990. Almost 70 percent bore only one child. Thus, the overwhelming majority of city women in this age group will have only one child to support them when they reach age 65 in the years 2021 to 2025. Town and rural women had better prospects. Town women who were aged 30 to 34 in 1990 had 1.53 children alive in 1990, while rural women aged 30 to 34 in 1990 had an average of 2.21 children alive in 1990. Qiao predicts further that younger couples in their 20s who have had children since 1990 will have even bleaker prospects for support from their children. This generation will become elderly in the decade between 2025 and 2035.

The prospective burden for single children—the "little emperors" of the one-child policy who receive lavish attention and dotage from their parents—is daunting. It is conceivable that if both the husband and wife are single children, they could be responsible for the care of four parents and maybe even more surviving grandparents. Even if Chinese sons and daughters want to care for their parents, they may find the burden too great. Since by tradition only the son is expected to take care of the parents, this could leave the parents of daughters in a bind if the daughters (and their husbands) are not persuaded to care for her parents.

The elderly in smaller cities and towns face difficult prospects, but they have more resources than in the urban areas. The level of social protection, however, is declining. There is pressure on SOEs to reduce benefits, and the non-SOEs generally provide no benefits or benefits at a much lower level than the SOEs. Many of the tens of millions who have been laid off have not been able to find new employment and may have lost full entitlement to their retirement benefits from their former employers. Although many have found new jobs, they have not gained new retirement and health care benefits with those jobs. The central government is concerned about the potential for urban poverty to increase and has taken steps to provide minimal public assistance for those in dire poverty, but the level of support is modest.

Profound change lies ahead. Hu Angang predicts that China will face three population peaks, each with its own policy implications. In 2020 China's working population will total around 1 billion. "That means we will have to create a lot of jobs," he told a World Economic Forum a few years ago.[45] The second peak will come in 2040, when 230 million Chinese will be 60 or older. By 2045, China's population is expected to reach its peak of 1.534 billion,[46] possibly making it more dependent on food imports.[47]

Thus, demographic trends from the perspective of aging show that the number of elderly in China will increase dramatically and rapidly. They will be concentrated in urban areas where they may constitute up to half the population of some cities. Parents without pensions in urban areas, where the one-child policy was followed strictly, may not have a son to support them. Rural offspring may have departed to the cities, throwing the rural elderly on the mercies of the local community. Those elderly who do manage to have a pension will not have the level of support that the state has historically provided. Even if China finds a way to finance the more streamlined social security system that survives its transition to a market economy, the real unmet needs of the elderly could be vast. Governments of all levels are likely to face demands that they provide support for the great majority of the elderly who will fall outside of the social safety net. With China's growing prosperity, the working-age population may be able to shoulder the increased social responsibility through higher taxes, but the state is also likely to face pressures to borrow funds to provide minimal income and health benefits.

Rural areas. China classifies 783.8 million of its people as rural, which means they live in the countryside or in villages. Towns are considered urban places. Although rural folk increasingly rely on income from collectives started up during the reform era, employment in these enterprises is, in fact, declining. Without any broad-based social security plan, most rural, elderly Chinese depend on their children for support, as they have throughout the millennia. The eldest son, by tradition, is expected to take care of his parents, while daughters are presumed to help their husbands take care of his parents. There is little doubt among demographers that the concern about old-age security is a key factor in the rising gender imbalance in China, especially in the countryside. The prospects facing the rural elderly prompted demographer Xiaochun Qiao to conclude that "the aging problem in rural areas [is] much more serious than that in urban areas."[48]

In the rural areas where there is no formal social security program outside of the family, except for a very modest voluntary program that began in 1995 and enrolled only about 2.8 percent of the rural population.[49] China also supports a rural social relief program for the indigent elderly who have no dependants, are not able-bodied, and have no money (known as the three noes). There is no government-sponsored retiree health care in rural areas. Working-age peasants have to pay their own medical expenses, and rural facilities and doctors are sparse. Rural China's oft-praised system of "barefoot doctors" and rural clinics has disintegrated over the past decade.[50]

Internal Migration

The extent of rural-to-urban migration in China over the coming years will determine how many elderly are left without family social services protection. The greater the rural-to-urban migration, the more likely there will be substantial numbers of elderly left in rural areas who are not receiving support from their children. The OECD has estimated there are 250 million to 275 million surplus workers in rural areas.[51] If there is not sufficient economic development near the areas where these people live, they could over time travel into the cities in the coastal and northeastern areas where China is experiencing its highest level of development.

The extent and timing of any mass migration will affect who bears the burden of caring for the aging—families or government. The more the people move from rural to urban areas—especially cities at a great distance from their point of origin—the more the government and local authorities will face a rising burden of caring for the elderly. Because part of the population will not have a social security income or may have only a small pension benefit, the working-age population will assume an ever-rising financial burden of caring for the elderly. Robert Holzmann, director of social policy at World Bank China, believes that China cannot afford to develop a full social security program for its rural elderly.[52] If the economy and government revenues continue to rise, he suggests, China may be able to afford a small income allowance for most of its elderly—those over 70 or 75—who might otherwise be marginalized because local communities cannot serve all the elderly who need support.

The economic effect of migration during the time of rapid aging is more uncertain. Without a steady inflow of young migrants, the urban economy will face an aging problem as severe as any of the worst cases in the developed nations. Researchers skilled in econometric modeling of the impact of aging in developed countries find that aging would tend to slow the rate of economic growth and even reverse it if the working population declines. Aging will also slow the pace of gains in living standards. The OECD, for example, found that the expected significant declines in the sizes of the workforces in the European Union and Japan would represent a 0.9 percent reduction in potential GDP growth per year for the period 2025–2050.[53]

For China, the situation is likely to be different. Both its urban economy and its overall economy will likely benefit from the migration of workers to the cities as long as the process goes on, according to Fan Gang, director of the National Economic Research Institute.[54] "The aging issue is less significant for developing countries than it is for developed countries, particularly countries like China with a large rural population and still in the process of industrialization," Fan states. The changing structure of employment (less rural and more industrial) will improve the overall productivity of the economy, he adds. As young migrants move from villages to cities, the productivity of these migrants jumps enormously as they shift from the agricultural to the industrial and service sectors. And, with migration on such a large scale, not only are the labor needs of the cities met, but the overall productivity of the entire economy is constantly rising as a result, Fan says. These more productive migrant workers will be in a position to better sustain their elderly parents because their incomes will be higher because they migrated, Fan contends. The process of industrialization will continue, he says, for at least the next 20 to 30 years and will involve 250 to 350 million workers.

Notes

1. Qiao, "From Decline of Fertility to Transition of Age Structure."

2. Ibid.

3. "The Data of 1995 One Percent Population Survey" (Beijing: China Statistical Press, 1997.)

4. Chen Shengli, *The Mortality Changes of China since the 1930s* (Beijing: China Population Press, 1993).

5. *Zhongguo 2000 nian renkou pucha ziliao* [Tabulation of the 2000 population census of the People's Republic of China] (Beijing: China Statistics Press, August 2002) 1: 570–572.

6. Qiao, "From Decline of Fertility to Transition of Age Structure."

7. *Zhongguo 2000 nian renkou pucha ziliao* 1: 572.

8. Ibid.

9. Ibid.

10. *Zhongguo 2000 nian renkou pucha ziliao* 3: 1696.

11. Author's interview with Xiaochun Qiao, November 7, 2002.

12. Xinhua News Agency, "Minister Outlines Population Growth Challenges," November 6, 1998.

13. Ibid.

14. The National Population and Family Planning Law was passed by the Standing Committee of the National People's Congress.

15. Tim Mitchell, "Guangzhou Firm on One-Child Rule," *South China Morning Post*, August 13, 2002, p. 7.

16. Damien McElroy, "China's One-Child Fines Rise," CNN Asia, October 30, 2002, from http://asia.cnn.com.

17. Mitchell, "Guangzhou Firm on One-Child Rule."

18. Ibid.

19. Ibid.

20. *China Statistical Yearbook 2003*, table 4.2.

21. Author's interview with Stuart H. Leckie, chairman of the Hong Kong Retirement Schemes Association, September 27, 2002.

22. Author's interview with Athar Hussain, October 2002.

23. Population projection from State Family Planning Commission of China, http://www.chinapop.gov.cn.

24. *Zhongguo 2000 nian renkou pucha ziliao* 1: 570–571.

25. Population projection from State Family Planning Commission of China.

26. Ibid.

27. Data from China Population Information and Research Center, November 2002, http://www.cpirc.org.cn/index.htm (Chinese), http://www.cpirc.org.cn/en/eindex.htm (English).

28. Ibid.

29. Ibid.

30. "China Faces the Challenge of an Aging Society," *Beijing Review,* July 16, 2001.

31. Ibid.

32. Ibid.

33. Estimates of premature deaths range from 18.48 million to 30 million. For analysis, see Mark Yuying, An Wei Li, and Dennis Tao Yang, "Great Leap Forward or Backward? Anatomy of a Central Planning Disaster," Centre for Economic Policy Research, London, March 2001, p. 3, mimeo.

34. For discussion of the more the 30 million deaths during the Great Leap Forward, see Jasper Becker, *Hungry Ghosts: China's Secret Famine* (New York: Free Press, 1997).

35. Xinhua News Agency, "Gender imbalance becomes serious problem in China," August 24, 2003, http://news.xinhuanet.com/english/2003-08/24/content_1042226.htm.

36. Population Reference Bureau, http://www.prb.org, November 7, 2002.

37. *Zhongguo 2000 nian renkou pucha ziliao* 3: 1681–1682.

38. Daniel Kwan, "Gender Imbalance Big Threat, Say Experts," *South China Morning Post*, September 24, 2002, p. 8.

39. Valerie M. Hudson and Andrea Den Boer, "A Surplus of Men, A Deficit of Peace: Security and Sex Ratios in Asia's Largest States," *International Security* 26, no. 4 (Spring 2002): 5–38.

40. Paul Wiseman, "China Thrown Off Balance as Boys Outnumber Girls," *USA Today*, June 19, 2002, p. 1.

41. Qiao, "From Decline of Fertility to Transition of Age Structure," p. 67.

42. Lin Jiang, "Parity and Security: A Simulation of Old-Age Support in Urban and Rural China," *Population Development Review* 20, no. 2 (1994): 423–448.

43. Lin Jiang, "Changing Kinship Structure and Its Implications for Old Age Support in Urban and Rural China, *Population Studies* 49, no. 1 (1995): 127–145.

44. Qiao, "From Decline of Fertility to Transition of Age Structure," pp. 67–68.

45. Cable News Network, "China at 2050."

46. Population projection from State Family Planning Commission of China.

47. Despite China's huge size, only 13 percent of its 9,326,410 square miles are arable.

48. Xiaochun Qiao, "Aging Issue and Policy Choices in Rural China" (speech to the twenty-fourth International Union for the Scientific Study of Population), Salvador, Brazil, August 20–24, 2001.

49. "Business Booms in China's Gray Market," *China Daily*, December 28, 2003.

50. Elisabeth Rosenthal, "Without 'Barefoot Doctors,' China's Rural Families Suffer," *New York Times*, March 14, 2001, p. 1.

51. OECD, *China in the World Economy.*

52. Author's interview with Robert Holzmann, director of social policy at World Bank China, November 27, 2002.

53. Dave Turner, Claudio Giorno, Alain De Serres, Ann Vourc'h, and Peter Richardson, "The Macroeconomic Implications of Aging in a Global Context," Economics Department working paper no. 193 (Paris: OECD, 1998), table 3, p. 47.

54. Author's interview with Fan Gang, director of the National Economic Research Institute and the China Reform Foundation, September 20, 2002.

3

China's Economy and Aging Society

Aging will be an obstacle to China's progress toward key national goals because of the demographic expectation that China will face a 30-year period of rapid aging beginning in 2010. China will age before it becomes even a moderately developed country and before it produces a significant middle class.[1] After 2020, the potential burdens of sustaining the elderly population will be substantial and will absorb resources that might otherwise be available to the working population.

A fair assessment of the impact of aging on China's economy depends on understanding the factors that are driving China's economic growth and its gains in per capita income. In 1980 the GDP was 451.7 billion yuan ($264.9 billion).[2] In 2003 the economy grew at a brisk 9.1 percent and reached 11.67 trillion yuan ($1.409 trillion).[3] Per capita income rose from 460 yuan ($269) in 1980 to $1,090 in 2003.[4] Thus, while the economy grew by 5.31 times, per capita GDP grew by 4.05 times (figure 3.1). At the Sixteenth Party Congress in November 2002, Premier Jiang Zemin forecast that by 2020 China's economy would nearly quadruple yet again to 35 trillion yuan ($4.2 trillion), and per capita income would rise by a similar amount.

Despite China's enormous progress in achieving economic growth and raising living standards since the reform era began in 1978, annual per capita income remained at $1,090 in 2003.[5] It varies widely among the provinces, from a low of $165 in Guizhou Province to a high of $1,330 in Shanghai, according to a

Figure 3.1. GDP Growth Outpaces Per Capita Gains

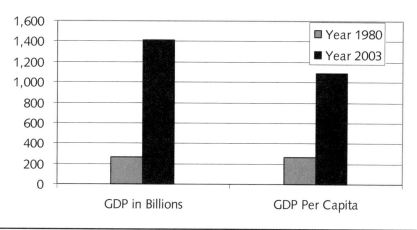

Source: *China Statistical Yearbook 2001*, tables 3-1, 17-2; National Bureau of Statistics.

2001 study of income classes by the China National Academy of Social Sciences (CASS).[6] About 229.5 million people—those who make at least $3,650 a year, 18 percent of the population—were classified by the study as middle-income earners,[7] which is not necessarily equivalent to the middle class.

In China, there is no official or widely accepted definition of what constitutes the middle class; the $3,650 level in the CASS study may be too low by standards in developed countries, even factoring in the fact that money goes a lot farther in China. For example, the Economist Intelligence Unit calculates that, on a purchasing parity basis, China's per capita GDP in 2001 was $4,302, not $911.[8] Other economists and sociologists define the middle class as people with higher family incomes—somewhere between $6,172 and $8,642 per year.[9] According to Liu Haoxing, the vast majority of the population can be classified as the working poor. The size of the population considered "moderately rich"—industrialists, investors, and businesspeople—is larger than the nation's middle class of professionals, bureaucrats, and managers.[10] The CASS study, edited by sociologist Lu Xueyi, divided China into five groups: the wealthy, the upper middle, the middle middle, the lower middle, and the poor. The number of people in the upper middle—Lu categorizes these people as wealthy—is greater than the number in the middle middle, which he sees as the middle class. Most people are in the lower middle group, and they are poor, noted Lu, but their incomes are "materially adequate."

Chinese officials are increasingly upbeat about the potential for economic gains in the coming decades. At the Communist Party's Sixteenth Congress in November 2002, former president Jiang Zemin set the goal of quadrupling the size of China's economy and providing similar increases in living standards for the Chinese people by 2020.[11] His goal for the year 2050 was an even more ambitious one of raising the average living standards of Chinese citizens to levels enjoyed by the world's most advanced countries, a goal that may, in fact, not be reached until 2100 or later.

China may well be in a good position to manage its transition to an aging society because it has only just begun to adopt productivity improvements that pervade developed countries. Economist Fan Gang explains that productivity is rising for two reasons: improved efficiency through investing in plant and equipment at individual enterprises, and the creation of new industrial jobs that draw in workers from the agricultural sector.[12] As workers who had very low productivity in the rural areas accept jobs in the cities, the country's overall productivity is rising, which potentially benefits the financing of the urban pension system to the extent that the firms hiring younger workers are included in that system.[13] Thus, Fan explains, the positive impact of economic development counters the negative impact of aging on the financial health of the nation's urban social security system: "The whole population is aging, but the [working] population [potentially] covered by social security is not aging, but is becoming even younger."[14] The rising productivity associated with the rural-to-urban migration also boosts the incomes of younger workers who have migrated from the countryside, thereby increasing their ability to support elderly parents.

Is China's Economy a Miracle?

The rapid development of China's economy after 1978 is viewed by some as a modern economic miracle. Yet, some doubt that this is the case. From time to time, there are hints that China's economy is all a bubble, that growth rates are vastly overstated, and that the economy is built on sand and will not last. Novel explanations have been offered for why the growth has occurred, including the speculation: Could China's gains so far be a function of changing demographics?

Effects of Demographic Change

Some economists have attributed a great many of the economic gains in East Asia—especially those in South Korea, Taiwan, Hong Kong, and Singapore—to a decline in fertility. This type of demographic shock, in fact, has a much stronger economic effect than the baby booms have had in the developed countries, Jeffrey G. Williamson argued in a 2001 paper for the Federal Reserve Bank of Boston.[15] In the developed world, a baby boom at first increases consumption at the expense of savings; but when the baby boomers reach adulthood, they produce a savings boom, which contributes to an economic miracle. Finally, baby boomers retire and push down savings rates and the economic miracle deflates.[16] The increase in saving that comes when the baby boomers reach adulthood coincides with an increasing need for investment in transportation infrastructure, capital goods, and housing. When there is a glut of elderly, saving and the demand for saving will decline.

Williamson contends that the same effect can occur in the developing world when a nation characterized by high fertility first experiences a significant fertility decline. The first working generation that has fewer children can save more, which drives up savings rates. Investment also rises and leads to an economic boom. In a 1997 paper, Higgins and Williamson set out to correlate changes in demographics with changes in savings, investment, and capital flows in 16 Asian nations[17] in the years between 1955 and 1992.[18] They found that as fertility rates declined (and as the working-age population continued to grow) domestic savings rates soared in Asia from 14 percent in the late 1950s to 35 percent in the early 1990s.

A similar turnaround occurred in capital flows. Between 1955 and 1959, the 16 Asian nations in the study by Higgins and Williamson imported capital equivalent to 4.86 percent of their combined GDP. By 1985–1989, capital outflows from the 16 had risen to 5.26 percent of GDP (table 3.1). Between 1990 and 1992, as the 16 Asian nations began to age, capital outflows fell to 2.38 percent for the years 1990 to 1992.[19] This illustrates the effect of demographic change on the economy: young nations import capital and old nations export capital, Williamson states. "If global capital markets are well integrated, and if pro-global policy lets it happen, capital tends to move between nations like an intergenerational transfer from old to young," he argues.[20]

Williamson has also examined the role that demographic change plays in economic growth rates, especially whether demography can explain much of East Asia's economic miracle. In a 1998 paper, Bloom and Williamson analyzed data from 78 countries[21] between 1965 and 1990 to come up with coefficients or equations that would explain the role of demographic change in economic growth.[22] They found that a 1 percent increase in the growth rate of the working-age population is associated with a 1.46 percent increase in the growth rate of GDP per capita. Conversely, a 1 percent decline in the growth rate of the dependent population is associated with a 1 percent increase in the growth rate of GDP.

Bloom and Williamson then applied these coefficients to the experience in East Asia between 1965 and 1990 and found that population dynamics explain between 1.4 and 1.9 percentage points of the growth in GDP per capita—or nearly one-third of the average 6.1 percent economic growth rate for the region (table 3.2). Looking forward, Bloom and Williamson predict that between 1990 and 2025 the aging of the population in East Asian nations will subtract 0.1 to 0.4 percentage points from economic growth rates—a net change in effect over the 1965–1990 period of 1.5 to 2.3 percentage points that is caused entirely by the impact of demographic change.[23] Since that range (1.5 percent to 2.3 percent) is for a group of nations that still have high fertility rates—like India, Pakistan, and Bangladesh—the effect on nations with sharp drops in fertility is likely to be much stronger. Williamson also contends that immigration from poorer young regions to richer older regions can raise living standards and growth rates for both. While China's rural areas have low fertility, their fertility rate is higher than it is in the cities and, thus, China's continuing rural-to-urban migration could offset the demographic effect that Williamson describes.

Table 3.1. Savings, Investment, and Net Capital Flows in Asia as Percent Shares of GDP, 1950–1992

Period	Savings (percent)	Investment (percent)	Current Account Balance
1950–1954	—	18.03	—
1955–1959	13.93	18.79	−4.86
1960–1964	18.26	23.53	−4.59
1965–1969	23.97	25.08	−3.39
1970–1974	28.97	28.50	−1.35
1975–1979	29.65	29.96	−0.67
1980–1984	28.62	29.14	−0.09
1985–1989	34.01	28.27	5.26
1990–1992	35.03	30.78	2.38

Source: Matthew Higgins and Jeffrey G. Williamson, "Age Structure Dynamics in Asia and Dependence on Foreign Capital," *Population and Development Review* 23 (June 1997): 267, table 3.
Note: Unweighted country averages.

Raymond Foo, Tham Mun Hon, and Winner Lee completed a major study of China's economy in 2002 for BNP Paribas Peregrine in Hong Kong; their study has shed further light on China's economic gains.[24] Foo, Hon, and Lee found that China's average economic growth rate has not been the fastest in Asia since 1978. It was, instead, number five—after Hong Kong, Singapore, South Korea, and Taiwan. They found that GDP per capita had not been keeping pace with gains in the economy because of an almost 80 percent depreciation in the yuan against the U.S. dollar since 1978. And, finally, they found that China's growth is likely to continue as it reflects a continuation of its trend of 3.7 percent annual gains in total factor productivity (TFP) from 1960 to 2000.

The authors dispute claims that China's economic growth is a miracle and is the fastest in the world because such claims mistakenly ignore the effect of inflation and currency movements to arrive at real growth rates. With GDP measures only, China's average annual growth rate since 1978 has been 9.6 percent a year, peaking at 14.2 percent in 1992 before slowing to a rate between 7

Table 3.2. Contribution of Demographic Change to Future Economic Growth, 1990–2025

| | Projected Growth Rate | | | Estimated Contribution | | | |
| | | | | 1990–2025 Four Models | | | |
	Population	Economically Active Population	Dependent Population	(1)	(2)	(3)	(4)
Asia	1.36	1.610	0.99	0.61	0.99	0.50	0.43
East Asia	0.43	0.200	0.87	−0.40	−0.14	−0.44	−0.38
Southeast Asia	1.29	1.660	0.63	0.83	1.10	0.73	0.62
South Asia	1.65	2.110	0.90	1.02	1.38	0.90	0.77
Africa	2.40	2.780	1.88	0.98	1.63	0.73	0.68
Europe	0.17	−0.004	0.48	−0.32	−0.16	−0.34	−0.29
South America	1.50	1.870	0.94	0.82	1.15	0.71	0.60
North America	1.28	1.330	1.21	0.21	0.65	0.11	0.10
Oceania	1.08	0.930	1.37	−0.22	−0.24	−0.31	−0.26

Source: David Bloom and Jeffrey G. Williamson, "Demographic Transitions and Economic Miracles in Emerging Asia," *World Bank Economic Review* 12 (September 1998): 444.
Note: The following list describes the four models:

(1) Measures the effect of the difference between the growth rate of the economically active population and the total population. Also based on a model that *excludes* initial life expectancy and two geographical variables: a tropics dummy and a ratio of coastline to land area.

(2) Measures the effect of the difference between the growth rate of the economically active population and the total population. Also based on a model that *includes* initial life expectancy and two geographic variables: a tropics dummy and a ratio of coastline to land area.

(3) Measures the effect when the difference between the growth rate of the economically active population and the total population is constrained to be equal, but of opposite sign. Also based on a model that *excludes* initial life expectancy and two geographical variables: a tropics dummy and a ratio of coastline to land area.

(4) Measures the effect when the difference between the growth rate of the economically active population and the total population is constrained to be equal, but of opposite sign. Also based on a model that *includes* initial life expectancy and two geographic variables: a tropics dummy and a ratio of coastline to land area.

and 8 percent a year. (Foo et al. estimate that China's official data overstate growth by about 1 to 1.5 percent a year because of faulty data collection methods.) Singapore came in second with an average growth since 1978 of 7.4 percent, followed by Taiwan at 7.4 percent, and South Korea at 6.9 percent.

Foo, Hon, and Lee argue, however, that per capita GDP is a better measure of economic growth because it takes into account inflation and currency movements. In this lineup, Taiwan ranks first with a per capita GDP in 2001 that was 7.8 times the level of 1978. Next is South Korea, at 6.3 times 1978; Singapore follows at 6.2 times 1978. China is a distant fifth; its 2001 GDP was only 4 times its 1978 level. Further, the authors note, China's growth pattern measured in GDP per capita does not match of Japan's stellar gains from 1970 to 1993, when Japan's economy grew an average of 14.3 percent a year and its GDP per capita measured in U.S. dollars rose more than 18 times.[25]

In absolute terms, China must go a long way to catch up with its Asian neighbors in per capita GDP. In 2001, Hong Kong was far and away the leader in East Asia and Southeast Asia, with a per capita GDP of $24,387, more than 24 times higher than China's $911. Singapore was next at $20,740, followed by Taiwan at $12,582, and South Korea at $8,858.

China's prospects for increasing its per capita GDP are good, Foo Hun and Lee conclude, because China should be able to continue its high performance in raising TFP; see table 3.3. In particular, China has shown it can make good use of capital to raise its TFP, which puts China in the inspirational-economic-miracle category instead of the perspiration-growth category, as defined by Paul Krugman a decade ago.[26] To make further gains, however, China will have to "move up the value-added ladder," according to Foo,[27] because countries with lower labor costs, like Vietnam, will be increasingly more attractive for textiles and toy manufacturing, two big industries that have favored China. By moving up the value-added ladder, China can also boost its workers' per capita income, the authors state.

Foreign Direct Investment

A study by the International Monetary Fund has examined to what extent foreign direct investment (FDI) is the key factor in producing China's "economic takeoff" and whether it might also explain the rising income inequality, at least in the short term.[28] The authors, Anuradha Dayal-Gulati and Aasim H. Husain, examined provincial variations of FDI, because FDI is usually the engine of technology transfer and economic takeoff. This approach seemed promising because market-oriented innovations in China have usually been tried on an experimental basis

Table 3.3. Total Factor Productivity, 1960–2000

Contributions from	GDP Growth Rate (%)	Capital (GDP)	Capital (%)	Labor (GDP)	Labor (%)	TFP (GDP)	TFP (%)
China	9.4	4.4	46.8	1.3	13.3	3.7	39.8
Hong Kong	7.3	3.1	42.3	2.0	27.6	2.2	30.1
Singapore	8.5	6.2	73.1	2.7	31.6	-0.4	4.7
South Korea	10.3	4.8	44.2	4.4	42.2	1.2	11.6
Taiwan	9.1	3.7	40.5	3.6	39.8	1.8	19.8
Japan	6.8	3.9	56.9	1.0	14.3	2.0	28.8
United States	3.1	1.4	45.2	1.3	41.5	0.4	13.2

Source: Raymond Foo, Tham Mun Hon, Winner Lee, "Behind the Bamboo Curtain," in chapter 5 of *China, the United States, and the Global Economy*, ed. Shuxun Chen and Charles Wolf (Santa Monica, Calif: Rand, 2001).

in one location—usually as the result of local initiative—before being adopted as national policy. The authors note that China's impressive economic growth rates since 1978 have coincided with large inflows of FDI, which they calculate have averaged $40 billion annually (about 5.5 percent of GDP in recent years).[29] During this time, per capita GDP widened to the point that by 1997 the richest province had a per capita income eight times larger than the income of the poorest one, which compares with six times larger in 1978. The widening income gap corresponds to a similar divergence in FDI, which accounted for 9 percent of regional GDP from 1993 to 1997 in the coastal region but only 1 to 2 percent of regional GDP in the western and southeastern regions.

Dayal-Gulati and Husain concluded that per capita income is converging to different steady-state levels in different areas of China and is correlated with variations in FDI investments. The relatively richer coastal, northern, and northeastern regions "were probably able to attract more FDI precisely because of their relative prosperity and, consequently, more developed infrastructure."[30] Dayal-Gulati and Husain also found that the prevalence of SOEs and high bank loan–deposit ratios tended to be associated with lower growth. In other words, regions that failed to attract

FDI were given favorable treatment in borrowing money from state-owned banks, but, because these funds were invested in money-losing or low-return businesses, there was less gain in per capita GDP in those areas.

The ability to continue to attract significant levels of FDI would appear to be the key to further per capita income gains in China. Indeed, some observers believe China's attractiveness to foreign developers could make it the global engine of the economy of the future. Frank-Jürgen Richter, former director of the World Economic Forum's Asia department, in a 2002 report on FDI from the United Nations Conference on Trade and Development (UNCTAD),[31] predicted that China would overtake the United States as the world's manufacturing engine within five years.

Not everyone agrees with such a rosy assessment of China's prospects. Nor does everyone agree that a high level of FDI is a sign of economic health. Harvard economist Yasheng Huang contends that the high level of FDI flowing into China is not a positive indicator and suggests systemic imperfection within the economy.[32] FDI is flowing, he claims, because official policies that allocate credit and favorable governmental treatment discriminate against domestic private companies. Official policies, which are only slowly changing, reflect a political pecking order for enterprises, at the top of which stand the inefficient SOEs. At the bottom are small, family-owned businesses.

High FDI levels are attractive because they can partially offset the disadvantage of China's highly fragmented economy, Huang argues. The economy is fragmented along provincial, county, town, and city lines—with each level of government likely to try to protect industries and businesses at its level against competition from other Chinese firms outside its region. This protectionism creates barriers to the flow of goods, capital, and labor across geographic boundaries and makes China "one country, thirty-one economies,"[33] Huang states, referring to China's 31 provinces. Signs indicate that fragmentation may be increasing, not decreasing. The average distance of a freight shipment in China, for example, fell from 395 km to 310 km between 1978 and 2000.[34] FDI becomes attractive in this fragmented economic environment because joint ventures can attract capital resources beyond the geographic bounds imposed on domestic firms without a foreign tie. When FDI is directed at goods that are destined for export and not distributed within China, it also avoids the problem of regional protectionism.

Differing Predictions

Students and observers of China hold starkly differing visions of China's economic future. For example, Princeton University economics professor Gregory C. Chow has said that China's economy will equal the U.S. economy by 2020 if China grows at 6 percent per year while the U.S. economy grows at 2.9 percent.[35] Naysayers, such as Oliver August, see a different picture. August charges that China's growth is increasingly driven by its growing budget deficits and mounting debt. August contends that China's economy has huge overcapacity and, as a result, is suffering from deflation, while the government is responsible for the mounting bad loans at state-owned banks.[36] Others are even gloomier. Instead of China being the engine of the world economy, it could be the next Argentina (where finances collapsed in late 2001), according to Gordon Chang.[37]

   Although it may be nearly impossible to resolve the wildly divergent views about China's future, it is probably safe to say that the Chinese economy will continue to grow at a strong rate, that per capita GDP will continue to rise, and that in the meantime Chinese authorities must deal with serious challenges: unemployment, the need for a stronger safety net, reforms to promote growth in rural areas, rampant corruption, banking debts, and long-term rising costs in the urban social security system. These are not unmanageable problems, but they require China's leaders to take some bold steps to adopt systemwide reforms in the coming years rather than make small adjustments and tinker around the edges.

Market Economy's Effects on China's Policies toward the Elderly

China's economic development and transition to a market economy are transforming social norms in a way that aggravates the social effect of aging in China. Economic change will weaken the ability of families to take care of China's elderly as they have for thousands of years. The result will be a rising tide of demands for more social protection for the elderly as young workers with families seek to separate themselves into households separate from their parents. This will be true in both the urban areas, where the elderly have wider access to the country's limited and fragmented social security system, and the rural areas, where a formal universal social security system does not exist and old people rely almost entirely on their sons and their sons' families for support and survival. The trend of forming nuclear families instead of multigenerational families under one roof runs counter to the needs of the elderly because as many as four parents and additional grandparents may depend on the income of one couple.

The defining question, then, is whether an aging population will slow China's transition to a developed country. Although an aging society will certainly be a drag on potential economic growth, its effects could be fairly weak in China's transition to a moderately developed country in the 2020s. Its effects could be a much greater hindrance to China's effort to become a fully developed country by the 2050s.

An aging population can affect the pace of economic development and the transition to a market economy. The problems of China's aging population make it all the more important that China's transition to a market economy proceed with all due speed; doing nothing can become very expensive. Aging increases the cost of sustaining the current social security system and poses retirement risks for those who have either lost their retirement benefits or face reduced benefits but may not yet be aware of it. Aging also makes meaningful social security reform urgent if China is to avoid an already costly program becoming even costlier. China is likely to face pressure to redistribute a portion of the gains from those who are benefiting disproportionately from economic development to those who are not. More specifically, there is an imperative to create sustainable social benefits under the new market system. The government will also have to continue to respond to the demands to provide a social safety net for those left behind in China's transition, both the abject poor of working age in both the rural and urban areas, as well as the elderly who are left without family support or retirement benefits.

The economic restructuring that has been sweeping China has pushed millions of workers out of the generous benefit system (albeit with very low pay) that they enjoyed in the SOEs, and many millions more are likely to be laid off permanently as the downsizing continues. The official category of laid-off workers, *xiagang zhigong*, which translates as "standing down," until recently reflected the workers' status as still attached to the enterprise. Now, however, the *xiagang zhigong*, along with all current and former SOE workers, are losing the iron-rice-bowl system of welfare benefits that was the hallmark of modern Communist Chinese industrial development.

Debate exists over China's state-owned assets, especially shares in the SOEs; some argue they belong to all Chinese people and not only to those in the cities. Currently, China plans to sell off its share of those resources and deposit the proceeds in a national social security fund, which will fund unemployment benefits and provide subsidies for shortfalls in the urban social security system. The fact that China's rural population is not benefiting from this arrangement has raised questions of social equity. Mao Yushi, in a paper presented in 2001, commented:

> The assets of SOEs are solely owned by Chinese citizens including the peasantry, due to their large contributions created by selling their farm products to the government at a very low price in the 30 years prior to the beginning of reform in 1978. If they are excluded from the reform of the pension system, it is very unfair.[38]

Private Sector's Importance since 2001

China's enterprises that are the freest from central planning and governmental interference have, since the mid-1990s, become China's engine of economic growth. In 1999, the sector of the economy that was identified as private sector and was not state-owned or collectively owned (often by towns and villages) produced 3.40 trillion yuan, 46 percent of China's industrial output of 7.35 trillion yuan (figure 3.2).[39] State-owned industry, which produced almost 80 percent of output in 1978, contributed only 32 percent, or 2.31 trillion yuan, in value to the economy in 1999. The former engine of the economy—collectives, both urban and

Figure 3.2. Industrial Output in China by Type of Enterprise, 1999
(output in billion yuan)

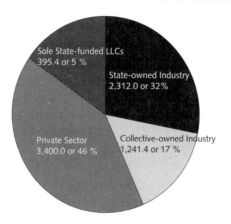

Source: Chart prepared from data found in *China Statistical Yearbook* 2001, table 13-1.

Note: Private sector includes cooperative enterprises, shareholding corporations, private enterprises, foreign-funded enterprises (plus Hong Kong, Macao and Taiwan), and limited liability corporations that are not solely funded by the state. The private category includes some state ownership. State-owned industry category includes joint ownership enterprises.

Figure 3.3. Industrial Output in China by Type of Enterprise, 2002
(output in billion yuan)

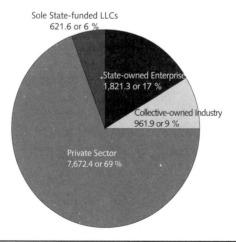

Source: Chart prepared from data found in *China Statistical Yearbook* 2003, table 13-1.

Note: See note to figure 3.2, above.

rural—produced 17 percent, or 1.24 trillion yuan, of China's industrial output. In 2000, the state-owned industry sector fell to 25 percent of industrial output as the collective sector shrank to 14 percent. Meanwhile the private sector zoomed to 56 percent, 4.82 trillion yuan of China's 8.57 trillion yuan industrial output.[40] Thus, 2000 was a watershed year for China when the private sector may have become the majority contributor to industrial output for first time since the founding of the People's Republic. This conclusion must remain tentative because many firms that can be classified as part of the private sector have some level of government ownership, directly or indirectly, and many—perhaps most—joint ventures still have a minority foreign partner. In 2001, the private sector's contribution to industrial output surged to 65 percent and in 2002 further increased to 69 percent, or 7.67 trillion of the nation's 11.03 trillion yuan output. Meanwhile the state-owned industry output fell to 1.82 trillion or 17 percent, while the output of collectives fell to 962 billion yuan or 9 percent (figure 3.3).

The private sector's dominance of the industrial sector is occurring as manufacturing continues to dominate China's economy. In 2001, for example, industry and construction accounted for 51.1 percent of China's GDP.[41] The service sector represented 33.7 percent, and the agricultural sector represented 15.5 percent.

Many international Western brand names are represented in China's private sector—McDonald's, Buick (General Motors), Starbucks, to name a few. There are also many small and medium-sized enterprises (SMEs) that are joint ventures with Chinese living outside mainland China, often in Hong Kong, Macao, Taiwan, and Singapore. One can see the relative size of these two segments of the FIE business sector in the employment numbers in table 3.4. In 2001, the FIE units with investment funds from Hong Kong, Macao, and Taiwan employed 3.26 million workers, while those from all other countries employed 3.45 million workers. Together, at 6.71 million, they still represented only 2.8 percent of the urban workforce. (The job numbers do not include Hong Kong.) The vast majority of private enterprises are individual businesses or very small businesses employing eight or fewer workers, typically family-owned. Even these businesses often have to have some sort of bureaucratic tie to government in order to function, according to Yasheng Huang.[42] "No one has witnessed the emergence of truly

Table 3.4. Composition of China's Workforce, 1998–2002

Employees (millions)	1998	1999	2000	2001	2002
Total employed persons	706.37	713.94	720.85	730.25	737.40
Urban employed persons	216.16	224.12	231.51	239.40	247.80
State-owned units	90.58	85.72	81.02	76.40	71.63
Urban collective-owned units	19.63	17.12	14.99	12.91	11.22
Cooperative units	1.36	1.44	1.55	1.53	1.61
Joint ownership units	0.48	0.46	0.42	0.45	0.45
Limited-liability corporations	4.84	6.03	6.87	8.41	10.83
Share-holding corporations	4.10	4.20	4.57	4.83	5.38
Private enterprises	9.73	10.53	12.68	15.27	19.99
Units with funds from Hong Kong, Macao, & Taiwan	2.94	3.06	3.10	3.26	3.67
Foreign-funded units	2.93	3.06	3.32	3.45	3.91
Self-employed individuals	22.59	24.14	21.36	21.31	22.69
Rural employed persons	490.21	489.82	489.34	490.85	489.60
Township and village enterprises	125.37	127.04	128.20	130.86	132.88
Private enterprises	7.37	9.69	11.39	11.87	14.11
Self-employed individuals	38.55	38.27	29.34	26.29	24.74

Source: *China Statistical Yearbook 2002*, table 5-1; *China Statistical Yearbook 2003*, table 5-1.

Note: From the urban total of 247.80 million employed in 2002, 153.47 million are identified by type of employment in official data; 94.37 million are not identified by type of employment. From the rural total of 489.60 million employed in 2002, 171.73 million are identified by type of employment in official data while 317.87 million not identified by type of employment.

private world-class firms owned and operated by the Chinese themselves," he writes. "Thus, their small individual size may suggest the presence in the Chinese economic system of substantial constraints on their ability to grow." Yet, paradoxically, they are proliferating and growing as a group, even as few large companies emerge from the group.

The emergence of the private sector of China's economy as the nominally majority sector—one that will likely grow dramatically in size and importance in the future—is clearly an important development. The state-owned sector—boosted by loans on favorable terms from state-owned banks—has not been able to make the kind of adjustment that will allow it to downsize and then grow again. Even though SOEs shed a stunning 36 million jobs,[43] or 32 percent of their workforce, from 1996 to 2001 (and more since), the SOE sector will likely continue to shrink as it struggles to be profitable. The collective sector lost 23.1 million jobs, 76 percent of its workforce, over the same five years. Clearly, market forces are powerfully reshaping China's economic landscape. This market dynamism—originally called creative destruction by free market economist Joseph Schumpeter—was described as "the churn" by Federal Reserve Bank of Dallas in a report on China a few years ago.[44] In fact, China's size led the president of the Federal Reserve Bank of Dallas, Bob McTeer, to call it "the mother of all churns."[45]

When one compares the number of industrial workers by type of enterprise with the industrial output from those workers, it is clear that the private sector is dramatically more productive. With 15.5 million workers, the private sector employed only 40 percent of China's 38.4 million industrial workers in 2001.[46] Yet, as noted, the private sector generated 56 percent of industrial output. The SOEs, by contrast, employed 18.2 million industrial workers, 47 percent of the industrial workforce. Yet, these workers generated only 18 percent of industrial output.

Economic Legacy of the State-Owned Enterprises

Many of China's big SOEs were set up in the 1950s and patterned after the former Soviet Union's industrial policy of huge investments for economic development and generous benefits for urban workers.[47] Sociology professor Nelson W.S. Chow believes that China's decision to copy the Soviet system was inappropriate because China was adopting a system that was too generous for a poor, backward country; this led China into the problems it has today. Generous urban social insurance benefits helped seal the political loyalty of urban workers but left rural people with nothing comparable. "But," Chow notes, "the price to be paid, not only in terms of the costs incurred in maintaining such a program, but also the discrepancies created between different categories of workers had certainly not been counted when the [Social Insurance] Regulations were introduced [in 1951 and 1953]."[48]

China's SOEs, as a group, remain bloated, and many are kept afloat through loans from state-owned banks and other forms of state help. The SOEs have been struggling to be profitable and some have succeeded, but the cost in terms of employment has been staggering. The industrial SOEs (both urban and rural) shed more than half their workers in only five years, falling from 42.78 million employed in 1996 to 18.24 million in 2001. The private sector, on the other hand, is lean, competitive, and growing in number of workers and output. The number of industrial workers in the private sector more than doubled from 1996 to 2001, rising from 7.43 million to 15.5 million.

Official Chinese statistics capture some, but not all, of the differences in efficiency between the state-owned companies and state holding companies as a group and the foreign-funded private sector. For example, in 2001, state-owned and state-held industrial enterprises reported overall labor productivity of 54,772 yuan per year.[49] By contrast, the overall productivity of foreign-owned enterprises (including businesses funded by capital from Hong Kong, Macao, and Taiwan) was a much higher 75,913 yuan per year in 2001.[50] The significant difference in annual labor productivity between SOEs and private businesses shows how workers in the private sector can outproduce workers in the state-owned sector.

Banking Reform

In addition to providing for the unemployed and creating a safety net of other benefits for the urban and rural poor despite the potential shortfall in the urban pension system, China must also deal with the cost of resolving bad loans on the books at four state-owned banks that dominate China's banking system. Partly as a result of commitments made in connection with China's entry into the World Trade Organization (WTO), this situation is changing rapidly and events and policies explained here may soon be out of date.

Banking reforms and restructuring could allow for a more rational and efficient allocation of an estimated 24.501 trillion yuan[51] ($2.960 trillion) deposited at financial institutions by businesses, organizations, and households. Funds in China's command economy were traditionally allocated by government leaders to SOEs. Since the reform era began in 1978, growing and dynamic non-SOEs have often been starved for capital. Despite reforms, funds available at banks continue to flow primarily to inefficient and sometimes bankrupt SOEs although efforts have been under way to make funds available to viable private business firms to borrow from the state-owned banks.

In 1984, the central government shifted responsibility for providing capital to SOEs from the state budget to the state-owned commercial banks. After 1984, bad loans began to accumulate quickly on the balance sheets of China's Big Four banks—the Bank of China, the Industrial and Commercial Bank of China, the Agricultural Bank of China, and the China Construction Bank—after government and party officials across the nation pressured the banks to make loans to SOEs. The SOEs were starved for capital because the central government began to reduce its huge subsidies to them and insist that they become self-sufficient and competitive with non-SOEs. By increasing loans to SOEs—and denying loans to more viable businesses—China has been promoting a vicious circle, the OECD charged in its mammoth 813-page China study.[52]

The banks continued to supply funds to money-losing enterprises, helping the central government preserve full employment in the cities, and "kept alive the illusion that China could avoid much of the pain of reform," according to Pieter Bottelier, former head of the Beijing office of the World Bank.[53] This approach to economic reform "bought time for people and institutions to adjust to the emerging realities of the market economy while incomes were growing and social stability was preserved," Bottelier adds.[54] The banks, in fulfilling this role, began to accumulate a growing portfolio of nonperforming loans. Beijing acknowledged the problem in 1999 when it transferred $171 billion in nonperforming loans from the Big Four and the State Development Bank to the four newly created asset management companies (AMCs) that were patterned on the concept of the Resolution Thrift Corporation in the United States after the savings and loan crisis of the late 1980s. The AMCs were to package the loans and sell them to investors. Yet the banks continue to make bad loans. The accumulated nonperforming loans at both the banks and the AMCs remain "the most pressing public finance problem that needs to be resolved," Bottelier says.

Just how big is the problem? Bottelier estimates that before the creation of the AMCs, the Big Four banks probably had nonperforming loans that represented 50 to 60 percent of their domestic loan portfolios.[55] Although this is a growing problem, it does not seem to be careening out of control because, although the magnitude of the nonperforming-loan problem in China continues to grow in absolute terms, it is not growing in relative terms. It appears to have peaked in 2000 as a portion of outstanding loans and as measured against the size of the overall economy.

In the early years after China acknowledged that it had a problem with bad loans, it was difficult to measure exactly the size of the problem. A somewhat clearer picture of the underlying values of the bad loans at China's banks emerged in April 2002 when the governor of the central bank revealed that nonperforming loans represented 25.4 percent of the Big Four's combined lending portfolio,[56] or 2.1 million yuan ($253.6 billion). By the end of September 2003, the Chinese Banking Regulatory Commission offered a rosier assessment of the situation: nonperforming loans totaled nearly 2 trillion yuan ($242 billion), but represented only 21.4 percent of all loans. This, however, reflected more a surge in overall lending than it did a reduction in nonperforming loans.

The central government's goal is to reduce nonperforming loans at its banks to 15 percent. Chinese regulators hope that once nonperforming loans are reduced to a more modest level, domestic banks can carry out successful IPOs to beef up their financial position and make them more competitive with foreign banks entering the Chinese market. In 2003 the Big Four banks made plans to launch IPOs both domestically and internationally beginning in 2005.[57]

A full measure of China's bad-loan problem must also include loans still on the books of the AMCs. The Chinese Banking Regulatory Commission reported that, as of March 2003, the four AMCs had sold 343.5 billion yuan of bad loans to mostly foreign banks. Of that amount, the AMCs had recovered 71.5 billion yuan, or about 21 percent, according to the central bank.[58] That still leaves the four AMCs—Huarong, Great Wall, Orient, and Cinda—with a significant portion of the original 1.4 trillion yuan ($170 billion) transferred to them in 1999, and most of these loans may be worth considerably less than the loans that have been sold. Meanwhile, more loans on the books at the Big Four may have become nonperforming but have not yet been identified as such by officials. Estimates of the total of nonperforming loans must also include those at other new banks created in recent years, including 11 national shareholding banks and 110 city commercial banks. With growth in lending at the new shareholding and city banks, the Big Four banks have been losing market share in recent years, falling from 70 percent of loans in 1999 to 44 percent in 2002.[59]

If one adds the official estimate of bad loans at the banks ($242 billion) to the remaining bad loans at the AMCs ($136 billion), one arrives at the minimal $375 billion estimate of the size of the problem. It is no surprise that several independent studies and estimates of the nonperforming-loan problem have yielded a higher number, $500 billion. For example, Ernst & Young estimated in 2001 that China's entire banking industry held $480 billion in unprofitable loans, or about 44 percent of total bank lending and 44 percent of the nation's GDP for that year.[60] In June 2003, Standard & Poor's estimated China's nonperforming loans at $500 billion, or 45 percent of total lending and 40 percent of the country's GDP.[61] Standard & Poor's analyst Ian Thompson cautioned that more bad news might be on the way: "[G]iven the brisk rate of loan growth over the past five years, the latent credit risk from loans extended in recent years could be high."[62] Bottelier also estimates that China has about $500 billion in nonperforming loans, of which he estimates that $400 billion is likely to remain unpaid.

The difference between official and nonofficial estimates may be due in part to that fact that Chinese banks have traditionally refrained from reclassifying a loan as nonperforming until the borrower had failed to make regular payments for two years. In the United States and in many developed countries, banks reclassify loans if a borrower has not made regular payments for 90 days. It is not clear whether the official method for classification of loans is based on the standard practiced by developed countries or is closer to the traditional method for classifying nonperforming loans at China's Big Four.

Some worry that China's efforts at bank restructuring, instead of resolving the crisis, may, in fact, work to perpetuate and aggravate it. For example, when the AMCs were created, they were given authority to borrow from the People's Bank of China, but their debts do not appear as part of official statistics measuring the nation's deficit. In 2000, for example, borrowing by the four AMCs added 4 percent to the national deficit, pushing it from an admirable 3 percent to a worrisome 7 percent of GDP, according to Nicholas Lardy.[63] He further calculated that, during 2000, 400 billion yuan in new loans were reclassified as nonperforming, enough to equal 4 percent of the GDP.

Bonin and Huang, in a 2001 study, found a number of flaws in the way China designed and set up the AMCs. They contend that because the organization of AMCs resembles the organization of SOEs, "the traditional problems associated with SOEs in China, e.g., shirking and corruption, will plague the AMCs."[64] Further, Bonin and Huang state that the one-on-one arrangement between each of the four AMCs and the Big Four banks "fosters collusive behavior and inhibits competition," which, in turn, creates a moral hazard.[65] They suggest that the parent bank that transferred loans to its AMC will, over time, come to see it as an outlet for future transfers. The central government will need to make a credible commitment that the transfer is a one-off policy in order to avoid this, Bonin and Huang state.[66] They also comment that employees at the AMCs lack the requisite skills to engage in the range of financial activities they have authority to carry out: loan recovery, venture capital activities, strategic consulting, and investment banking. By granting the AMCs the ability to engage in debt-equity swaps, China has made them vulnerable to industrial policy, the authors further charge.

Signs are worrisome that the early discipline that the Big Four attempted to apply to new lending in 1999 weakened during late 2002 and early 2003. Standard & Poor's estimates that overall loan growth at China's banks rose 23.6 percent year-over-year from June 2002 to June 2003, to reach 16.73 trillion yuan ($2 trillion).[67] A 31 percent growth of lending far outstripped the growth of the GDP from mid-2002 through September 2003, according to Nicholas Lardy. By contrast, lending grew at a 14 percent pace in the year before the big upsurge. "In every financial system, when loan growth accelerates dramatically, credit quality goes down," Lardy has said.[68]

In late 2003 the central government, signaling an acceleration of banking reforms, formed a new working group to help lead the Big Four banks to the capital market. In January 2004 the Ministry of Finance announced it had injected $45 billion into two of its banks to shore up their liquidity and prepare them for share offers on foreign stock markets.[69] The Bank of China has reported it received $20 billion of the government bailout.[70] The move was seen as strengthening the bank in advance of its plans to launch an IPO in 2005, and the bank has indicated that it believes the move will reduce its bad-loan ratio from 18 percent to below 10 percent. The China Construction Bank received a $25 billion capital injection.[71] The press reported that the central government was preparing to write off a $41 billion stake in the same two banks to further strengthen their balance sheets.[72]

China can benefit in many ways if it resolves its bad-loan problems. Resolution could smooth the way for a successful conclusion for its economic transition as well as for further banking reforms and restructuring that allow for a more rational and efficient allocation of an estimated 17.917 trillion yuan[73] ($2.164 trillion) in funds deposited at financial institutions by businesses, organizations, and households. A more rational allocation of those funds could help counter the possible short-term negative effect of bringing stronger credit discipline to China's bank lending. During 2003, overly expansive bank lending contributed to an oversupply of automobiles, consumer goods, aluminum, property, and telecommunications equipment, driving down prices and cutting into profits.

The central bank in 2003 raised reserve requirements and banned some loans. In April 2004 China further raised reserves and asked its banks to stop all new lending until early May. It is reported that the government is also considering regulations that forbid lending by commercial banks to China's many small automobile manufacturers and also forbid funding by local governments of the construction and expansion of automobile plants.[74] By September 2004, the central bank was looking at whether further measures might be needed to cool the economy—partly overheated by rapid credit growth. A more rational lending regime at China's banks could lead to a more rational allocation of loans that could create more sustainable and profitable growth.

Provided China addresses adequately the pressing reforms needed to further the restructuring of its SOEs and its banking system, the country is expected to be able to continue the rapid gains it has made since 1978 in per capita income. Per capita GDP has zoomed in China from $267 (417 yuan) per year in 1980[75] to $1,090 in 2003.[76] Future gains will rest on continued investment in improving productivity and continued high economic growth rates. If the expected benefits materialize, children in the future will enjoy a higher living standard when they become adults and will thus be better able to support their elderly parents. The government, too, will be better able to afford the benefits needed by those who will be left without support and pay costs associated with bad debts at banks and the shortfall in the social security system.

Financial Markets

Beyond the problems facing the banking sector, China also needs to address problems in its financial sector. Its markets are immature and plagued by legal and illegal stock manipulation and speculation. The markets are short on major institutional market players with the long-term risk-management and investing skills needed to strengthen and stabilize the markets. The market is so thin that enterprises rely almost entirely on bank lending and not the issuance of equity to raise capital. In 2001, for example, while 100 million yuan was raised in equity issues in China's markets, 1.3 trillion yuan was lent by its banks—a level 13 times higher.[77] The market capitalization of firms listed on China's exchanges is about the same as that of Hong Kong. Bond issues by enterprises are few and far between.

   The government treasury bond market is also uneven, with little investor interest in long-term bonds. In September 2002, for example, the People's Bank of China bought back 5 billion yuan[78] of 30-year Chinese treasury bonds—one-fifth of these securities then on the market—because the interest rates were so low and the market so illiquid. "Given the low rates and yields on these long-term bonds, trading has been quite thin for China's long-term markets," explained Zhu Jianhua, an analyst with China Securities Company in Beijing.[79] As a result of its weak bond market, the yield curve in China is often an anomaly.

   Institutional investors could become a positive force for deepening and strengthening the country's financial markets if China succeeds in advancing pension reform that provides real funding in the individual accounts created in 1995. For now, most have turned out to be notional accounts because funds that were supposed to be deposited in individual accounts have instead been redirected to pay for current benefits in the pay-as-you-go system. Investment choices for funds that actually accrue in individual accounts are made not by individuals but by local social security bureaus on behalf of funds pooled from many enterprises, sometimes at the local township level and sometimes at the provincial level. Enterprise supplemental pensions, which represent about 5 million employees,[80] could help develop the kind of institutional investor base that could bring sophisticated investing and valuations to China's volatile markets—if and when these funds become larger. To the extent that China develops a prefunded pension system, functioning markets can help provide the returns needed to reduce the burden on current workers; this in turn could help raise living standards.

Government Debt

Bad bank loans are only one piece—albeit one of the largest pieces—of the larger puzzle that constitutes China's implicit and contingent public sector debts. How big are all of China's financial obligations? Does China have the fiscal capability—through taxes, borrowing and asset sales—to meet those obligations? Former World Bank Beijing office chief Pieter Bottelier has examined the question of whether or not the Chinese state is solvent and found "no risk" that the central government would be unable to meet its external obligations.[81] However, Bottelier could not vouch for the ability of various components of the Chinese state—SOEs and local and provincial governments—to meet China's internal obligations. Some SOEs have defaulted, and several local governments have failed to pay employees' wages and pensions and their suppliers for goods and services. Thus far the central government has been able to meet the obligations of the lower level components of the state, but it cannot continue to do so indiscriminately without creating a moral hazard and producing inflationary pressures.

Solvency is a concern in China because of the extraordinary costs of financing the country's economic transition. Bottelier in table 3.5 roughly calculated the transition debt, and in table 3.6 did the same for China's transition assets.

This simplified balance sheet, Bottelier states, suggests that the central government has the capacity to finance its nonpension

Table 3.5. China's Transition Debt (in billions)

Debt	Yuan	Dollars
AMC bonds	800	96.7
Policy bank bonds	600	72.5
Remaining nonperforming loans	2,800	338.3
Debt to the central bank	600	72.5
SOE recapitalization needs	1,200	150.0
Local government debt	800	96.7
Total liabilities	6,800	821.6
Estimated present value	3,800	459.1

Source: Pieter Bottelier, "Managing China's Transition Debt: Challenges for Sustained Development," mimeo., Washington, D.C., November 7, 2002, pp. 13–14.

Note: The exchange rate in January 2004 was 8.2767 yuan for each U.S. dollar.

Table 3.6. China's Transition Assets (in billions)

Assets	Yuan	Dollars
Value of shares in listed SOEs	3,600	435.0
Market value of SOEs to be listed	2,300[a]	277.9[a]
Other marketable assets	400	48.3
Cash value of nonperforming loans and AMC sales	300	36.2
Total assets	6,600	1,232.0
Estimated present value	5,400	652.4

Source: Bottelier, "Managing China's Transition Debt."

[a] In the next five years.

Note: The exchange rate in January 2004 was 8.2767 yuan for each U.S. dollar.

transition debt from assets, provided asset market values do not collapse, the stock of the nonperforming loans does not grow much bigger, and the government is willing to sell all or most of the transition assets it holds.[82]

The fact that so much of China's transition assets are to be found in nontradable public sector shares in listed SOEs complicates the task of financing China's economic transition. If it were not possible to trade or mobilize a sufficient portion of the market value of the shares, China could rely instead on financing its transition debt by borrowing the funds and paying interest on the debt. For China, these options carry with them major policy changes. In deciding whether to borrow funds or sell assets to finance transition debt, China will be making decisions that will greatly change the role of the central government in the economy, Bottelier notes. If China relies primarily on selling assets, the state's ownership role in China's economy will be sharply reduced. Bottelier suggests that, although it is preferable in principle to reduce the state's role because that is in line with reform objectives, the optimal approach might be to combine asset sells with borrowing. One key reason is that China must also address the other big question: paying for the cost of implicit pension debt.

Bottelier's simplified balance sheet shows that the bottom line goes from slightly black to heavily red when the present value of China's unfunded pension obligation, which Bottelier estimates to be 4.5 trillion yuan ($543.7 billion) is added. The addition of the implicit pension debt brings China's total economic and social transition costs to 8.3 trillion yuan ($1,002.8 billion), a figure far greater than the 5.4 trillion yuan in transition assets available to cover those costs. Bottelier notes: "If the implicit pension debt is included in the transition debt, the table suggests that the state faces a potentially serious solvency problem."[83]

When he analyzes China's solvency, Bottelier prefers to separate the transition debt from the implicit pension debt, partly because the pension obligation is something that will be paid out over many years. Also, the price tag for the implicit pension debt could be reduced by changes to the design and parameters of the pension system. Benefits could be further reduced and new revenue sources provided to protect the solvency of the state, Bottelier suggests. He also separates the two for policy reasons, noting that the government tried in 2000 and 2001 to fund up front its implicit pension debt through asset sales and encountered difficulties when share prices fell sharply on news of the government's sale of assets. Instead of resuming the sales in July 2002, the government chose to permit foreign agents to acquire majority interests in SOEs listed on domestic stock exchanges. Such acquisitions must be negotiated outside the exchanges, and new owners have to agree to hold the shares for an extended period before reselling them.

Bottelier also suggests that the government use the value of its assets to issue new financial instruments to finance the transition debt, thereby allowing the state to finance the transition debt without depressing the value of shares. Before such instruments could be offered, the central government would have to make legislative changes to ensure that asset-backed securities are freely tradable and that holders of the debt would have quick access in the event of a default, Bottelier states.

The task ahead is daunting. "The financial tightrope that China's government will have to walk in the coming years presents enormous challenges," Bottelier states.[84] To resolve the transition debt problem successfully, China will have to pursue further bank and SOE reform as well as take additional steps to develop its capital markets. It will have to build confidence in the market and broaden the range of its financial instruments while avoiding a stock exchange collapse. The government must avoid a too rapid withdrawal of deposits from its banking system, which would undermine the liquidity of the state banks. Because the state-owned banks are likely to continue to play a major role in the economy, Bottelier suggests that breaking some of them into smaller units might permit them to be reformed at different speeds, depending on their location and the management skills of their staff. This would also advance recapitalization and privatization of SOEs.

Unemployment

As China moves toward what it calls a "socialist market economy with Chinese characteristics," it is counting on the job creation ability of the market economy to provide new jobs to make the transition as free as possible from social and labor unrest. It is a daunting task. Not only must the private sector create jobs to replace the jobs lost in the downsizing of the SOEs (and, increasingly, of the industrial collectives as well), it must also create jobs for the 10 million new entrants expected in the urban labor force each year—the number of new workers will continue to increase until about 2025, when it will begin to decline. Jobs will also be needed for the huge inflow of migrants, both legal and illegal, to the cities. Good jobs are also needed in rural areas to address the widening gap in income between urban and rural China. To create these jobs, China's economy must grow at a brisk pace or China will face potentially destabilizing levels of social unrest.

China's official urban unemployment rate is low; for example, it stood at 4.3 percent (7.93 million) in September 2003. The number is misleading, however, because it tallies only those who have registered as unemployed (*dengji shiye ren yuan*). It does not include laid-off workers (*xiagang zhigong*), whose numbers are tallied separately. The number of laid-off workers was 3.1 million in September 2003. Together the unemployed and laid-off workers represent 11.03 million working-age people or 6.0 percent of China's estimated 185 million urban workers in the formal sector (table 3.7).

Rising unemployment in urban areas prompted the MLSS to say that China needed an additional 24 million urban jobs in 2003 alone.[85] These jobs were needed for 10 million young people who had entered the urban labor market during the year, 6 million laid off from state-owned and collectively owned firms, and nearly 8 million jobless residents registered with government labor agencies.[86]

A number of nongovernment economists have suggested that the real unemployment rate is probably closer to 7 percent or 8 percent in the formal sector. British economist and China expert Athar Hussain, of the London School of Economics, has estimated the unemployment rate as 12.4 percent by counting only full-time workers.[87] Layoffs in such places as Daqing, Laoyang, and Chongqing sparked huge protests in 2002. Zeng Xiangquan, president of the School of Labor and Personnel at the Renmin University of China, commented in 2003 that most Chinese labor experts believe China's unemployment rate has reached 10 to 15 percent and will continue to rise in the coming years.[88] Unemployment in some big cities—Fuzhou, Shanghai, Shenyang, Xi'an, and Wuhan—has been double the level reported for the nation.[89]

The central government has announced plans to pursue policies to accelerate economic growth in a bid to increase the number of new jobs created. Minister of Labor and Social Security Zhen Silin has set the 2004 target for new jobs at 9 million—an official unemployment rate target of 4.7 percent. That's one million more jobs than the economy created in 2003 but not enough to avoid a modest boost in the official projection in unemployment.

Official unemployment numbers are likely to jump after the end of 2004, when the government phases out programs for an

Table 3.7. Unemployment Funds, 1997–2002

	1997	1998	1999	2000	2001	2002
Number of unemployed city/town workers at year end (in millions)	5.8	5.7	5.8	6.0	6.8	7.7
Percentage registered for unemployment benefits	3.1	3.1	3.1	3.1	3.6	4.0
Number of participants for unemployment benefits elig-ible at year end (in millions)	79.6	79.3	98.5	104.0	103.6	101.8
Income of unemployment benefit funds (in billions yuan RMB)	4.7	7.3	12.5	15.9	18.9	21.6
Expenditure of unemployment benefit funds (in billions yuan RMB)	3.6	5.6	9.2	12.5	16.0	18.7
Accumulated surplus of unemployment benefit funds (in billions yuan RMB)	9.7	13.3	16.0	19.2	22.0	25.4
Number of laid-off workers of state enterprises (in millions)	—	6.0	6.5	6.6	5.2	5.2
Number of reemployed workers (in millions)	—	6.1	4.9	3.6	2.3	1.3

Sources: Data from *China Statistical Yearbook 2001*; *China Labor Statistical Yearbook 2003*, tables 2-2, 2-8, 2-10, 11-25, and 11-31; and statistics of the Ministry of Labor and Social Security.

estimated 3.1 million laid-off workers and those workers who have not yet found employment are reclassified as unemployed. A number of factors will add to the ranks of the unemployed, according to Zhen. The country will face a rising oversupply of labor as the number of new job seekers entering the market is expected to average 15 million per year between 2004 and 2020. The economy must grow at least 7 percent annually to create 8 million jobs per year, Zhen adds. In addition, the ranks of the redundant and the unemployed will swell as more unprofitable SOEs continue to close down or go bankrupt during the process of economic restructuring. Economic growth, while necessary to boost employment numbers, is not as powerful a job growth engine as it once was. During the 1980s a one-percentage-point increase in GDP led to 2.4 million new jobs, but during the 1990s this declined sharply to 700,000 for each percentage point of economic growth.[90]

An official white paper released by the State Council in April 2002 predicted that the ranks of the unemployed would triple to 20 million in four years, creating what the Vice Minister of Labor Wang Dongjin called the most serious unemployment pressures China has ever faced.[91] This as well as other warnings and reports throughout 2002 and 2003 appear to be preparing the public for tough times ahead.

In June 2002 the Chinese Academy of Social Sciences released a semiofficial green paper that predicted that China's jobless rate would rise above a "critical point" or "warning level" of 7 percent, where it might lead to serious social unrest.[92] The estimate came from a survey of more than 50 well-known scholars who engage in research on employment and labor issues.[93] Nearly three-quarters of the experts surveyed expect the unemployment level to increase by 1 to 2 percent in the next few years as Chinese enterprises face increased competition as a result of China's accession to the WTO.

The ranks of the jobless are increasingly younger. A 62-city survey by the Institute of Labor Studies within China's MLSS found that unemployment is increasingly concentrated among workers 35 and under. In June 2002, the survey found that, compared with less than 50 percent in 2000, 60 percent of the jobless were 35 and under.[94] "The younger age of the jobless serves as major proof that the country is facing a serious labor oversupply" [or job shortage], according to the author of the report, Mo Rong.[95] Mo predicts not only that unemployment will continue to rise but that it will increasingly be made up of young people.

Although employment prospects remain excellent for the well-educated in China, they are challenging for the great numbers of young workers entering the labor force every year. Since 2000, 12.4 million young workers have entered the labor force each year, a pace that is expected to continue through 2005. China's economy will likely not be able to grow fast enough to create the number of jobs needed to absorb the new labor entrants— to say nothing of those who have exited the workforce because of layoffs.

The influx of new young workers reduces the rate of reemployment of laid-off workers. In 1998, 50 percent of laid-off workers were reemployed. In 1999, it was 42 percent; in 2000, 35 percent; in 2001, 30 percent; and in the first half of 2002, 9 percent.[96] Coupled with this problem are the migrants pouring into the cities who are not counted in any of the official numbers but who need jobs. When they remain unemployed, they add to the ranks of the abjectly poor.

One government official has estimated that to keep the unemployment rate from rising, China's economy will need to create an additional 17 million jobs a year,[97] 9 million more than officially predicted under the assumption of a 7 percent annual economic growth rate. During the period 2002–2005, that would create a shortfall in jobs of 27 million. The situation will be so dire, economist Hu Angang told *Time,* that it will lead to "an unemployment war, with people fighting for jobs that don't exist."[98]

The need to create new jobs has led Chinese authorities to place more faith in the continued success and expansion of the vital and growing private sector. At the Sixteenth Party Congress in 2002, former minister of labor and social security, Zhang Zouji, credited the private sector with creating 30 million urban jobs between 1990 and 2001 while the SOEs lost 25 million jobs.[99] Increasingly, these jobs are going to be in the service sector, which has increased its share of total urban jobs from 18.5 percent in 1990 to 27.7 percent in 2001, Zhang reported.[100]

The ranks of the unemployed are likely far larger than official and semiofficial estimates—even the most dire and grim—because China counts as unemployed or laid off only those who are registered for unemployment, *dengji shiye ren yuan.* Only a small fraction of the 130 million or more migrants from rural areas who now live in cities are part of official data on unemployment; these are people who have permission under the *hu kou* system to live in the cities. The *hu kou* functions as an internal passport; China's citizens must have official permission to move from their places of birth to other locations. Those who move without permission are considered illegal migrants.

British economist Athar Hussain contends that China's true unemployment should include all those people who are currently without jobs and are looking for jobs. Hussain defines a job as a position that provides an income at least equal to the local poverty line; in most instances, this means a full-time job. Using 2000 data, Hussain calculates that the total of registered unemployed and laid-off workers of 14.6 million in 2000 officially was 7.6 percent of the nonemployed urban labor force of 191 million.[101] He claims, however, that the denominator, 191 million, in that calculation is too large because it includes workers—temporary workers, those informally employed, and private sector employees—who would never be classified as either registered unemployed or laid-off workers if they were to lose their jobs. The temporary, informal, and private sector workers are outside the scope of unemployment benefits and, thus, are not eligible for unemployment compensation should they be laid off. If those workers are not included in the 191 million, the denominator becomes only 118.5 million. Thus, 14.6 million unemployed would amount to a 12.3 percent unemployment rate.[102]

Hussain does not venture to estimate the unemployment rate among workers who work at firms that are not part of the unemployment benefits program, but he suggests that unemployment in this group is probably as high as it is in the formal sector, and perhaps higher. If that is true, the total number of urban unemployed would be closer to 30 million. Also, with Hussain's methodology, the unemployment rate in some troubled cities—those now reporting very high registered unemployment and high levels of laid-off workers—can be estimated at probably 20 percent or higher.

Social Problems Caused by Unemployment. Growing unemployment in urban areas has raised concerns that urban poverty could increase. The Ministry of Civil Affairs, which oversees urban poverty relief, conducted a survey in 2000 and found that 14 million urban residents with incomes below local poverty lines, 10 million of them were employed.[103] In January 2002, the All-China Federation of Trade Unions reported from its own study that there were 18.28 million urban workers with incomes below the poverty line.[104] In March 2002, the Xinhua News Agency reported that there were 30 million poor people in Chinese cities.[105] The poverty line, as noted earlier, is really a measure of abject poverty. In Beijing, for example, the poverty line is 285 yuan per month, but the minimum wage is 435 yuan per month.[106]

Rural unemployment and underemployment (holding only a part-time job) is almost impossible to measure, researchers say, and rural joblessness is not officially counted. The OECD, however, has estimated that unemployment and underemployment in China is somewhere between 200 million and 275 million out of the government's officially reported 350 million agricultural workers.[107] Some of these might be holding part-time jobs, according to the OECD.

The Widening Income Gap. In recent years, as the urban areas have been able to improve per capita income, the rural areas increasingly have not been able to keep up. For one thing, the job engine of the town and village enterprises (TVEs) that gave rural areas such dynamism in the early years of the reform era has run into a dry spell since the mid-1990s. Further, farmers, whose incomes were already under pressure, are facing increasing competition under the rules of the WTO. The lack of significant new economic development in the rural areas will continue to drive more rural residents into the cities in search of employment. This fuels resentment and widens the division between rural and urban China.

In late 2001 a study by China's Academy of Social Sciences found that the richest 20 percent of Chinese households are 4.5 times better off than the poorest.[108] In 1978, the richest quintile was 2.7 times richer than the bottom quintile. China's urban-rural gap, which shrank during the 1980s, has widened to a historical high.[109] Since urban incomes are growing faster than rural incomes, this gap is expected to widen. In 2001, the average annual income of urban residents was 6,860 yuan, and it was growing at 8.5 percent a year, according to official reports. The average annual income of rural residents was 2,366 yuan, and it was growing at 4.2 percent a year.[110] Officials are increasingly concerned and are willing to publicly discuss this growing disparity. In 2002, for example, former premier Zhu Rongji said that the gap between the rich and poor in China was reaching the "international danger level," meaning that the differences in income between the lowest wage earners and the highest wage earners were at levels that have historically ignited social conflict.

Few academics in China have done as much to sound the alarm about China's growing income gap than economist Hu Angang, director of the Center for China Studies under the auspices of the Chinese Academy of Sciences at Tsinghua University. In his book, *China Strategic Concepts*, he contends that since 1992 farmers have been falling behind as China continues to reform its economy. He finds that the income gap between rural and urban China declined in both absolute and proportional terms from the beginning of the reform era until about 1992. Since 1992, however, the rural-urban gap has widened.

Hu describes China as "one country, two systems, but four societies." The two systems are rural and urban China, which differ in residency control, education, employment, public services, and taxation systems. China's four societies are farming, manufacturing, services, and knowledge (technology, education, health, finance, business, and the civil service). Hu recommends that to narrow the gap between urban and rural areas, the central government needs to accelerate policies that promote urbanization; invest more in the poor western provinces; and speed up the development of the manufacturing, service, and knowledge sectors.

The central government increasingly hopes that the private sector will accomplish many of the goals that Hu has identified. The government has taken several steps in this direction, beginning with welcoming capitalists into the Communist Party in late 2001—a policy ratified at the Sixteenth Party Congress in November 2002. This is partly in recognition of the vital role that the private sector plays in China's economy and also to help decrease the differences between SOEs and collective enterprises and the private sector.

At the Sixteenth Party Congress, Zeng Peiyan, the minister in charge of the State Planning Commission, described the 13 years since 1989 as "the best development period in Chinese history"[111] and "a prosperous golden age" in which the masses of China enjoyed advances in their living standards. Zeng announced that China would take steps to remove barriers for the dynamic private sector so that the marketplace would be more competitive. "Private enterprises will be treated the same as state-owned enterprises and foreign-invested enterprises (FIEs) in market access, use of land, taxation, credit, and foreign trade," Zeng said.[112] Officially this means that they will have the same chances at getting bank loans as the SOEs, which currently get most of the loans. It also means that tax-favored FIEs will see their tax preferences phased out. Domestic private enterprises, if they can show sufficient financial strength, may have access to the bond markets. In practice, however, provincial and local authorities may continue to impose their will on how credit is allocated, and China's investors may resist buying corporate bonds in view of the lack of transparency in companies and questions about regulatory oversight.

Personal Savings

The industrialization process depends, of course, on attracting investment capital to start up the enterprises that will employ the great migration of rural people to urban areas. The potential of 250 million to 350 million new nonagricultural jobs will also depend on how well China's interior provinces in the West, South and Northwest attract capital, according to Holzmann at the World Bank.[113] So far, both FDI and domestic investment have favored the coastal, southeast, and northern areas of China. Thus, without better distribution of investment, some provinces may continue to industrialize rapidly while others do not. If migration to cities does not occur, China may need its urban elderly to work longer, beyond the current retirement ages of 60 for men, 50 for nonsalaried women, and 55 for salaried women, which are low by international standards, Holzmann suggests.

In China, the high savings rate of 40 percent of GNP, according to official macroeconomic data, does not necessarily translate to high household saving.[114] Studies of micro data on household saving in China have found a very low overall savings rate of 1.71 percent for urban households in 1995, with only 29 percent of households saving at a rate of 20 percent or more, according to Noriyuki Takayama.[115] This low savings rate suggests workers in China will not accumulate a lot of savings for retirement and "the majority of the people in the People's Republic of China would be obliged to rely heavily on social security pensions after retirement."[116] What China does have is a large pool of deposits that could be better allocated toward profitable non-SOEs that can provide sustainable growth.

Researchers find that aging populations save less (some claim the elderly actually dissave.)[117] Will this lead to a lower rate of saving in China? Conventional wisdom would say yes, but Fan believes that the patterns affecting developed nations will not affect developing nations, especially China. The same mass migration of rural young people to urban areas for jobs will also drive up savings rates because people in rural areas, who often have very low incomes, save very little if at all. When young people move to cities, they will be able to save for the first time. The entry of tens of millions of new savers into the economy will drive up aggregate savings and overall savings rates, Fan says. Even if the savings rate falls from 40 percent to 20 percent because of aging, the effect of migration will be greater. "The force of saving by the migrants could overwhelm any force of dissaving" Fan says.[118]

Will aging make the economic challenges facing China more difficult? Most observers believe the answer is "yes" if China fails to deal with immediate problems such as further restructuring of the economy and the banking sector, the development of income support where it is needed on a level that the central government can afford, and a reform of the pension system so that it is sustainable during the accelerated aging of China's population. Even if the challenges of unemployment, the income gap, the underfunded pension system, and the banking sector are adequately addressed, however, aging will still pose a challenge to China's fiscal health and its hopes for prosperity.

Notes

1. The fact that more people are scrambling for better health care and so few—fewer than 20 percent in rural areas, although in urban areas the coverage is much higher—are covered under any social security program would seem to put the problems of aging in China in a category very different from the situation in developed countries. Often the focus in developed and even some developing countries is how to devise ways to improve the prefunding of retirement benefits to increase the overall national savings rate in order to invest more in the nation's economic development, thereby giving future workers and governments more resources to pay for the burden of social benefits for the elderly.

2. *China Statistical Yearbook 2001*, table 3-1, p. 49. Yuan for 1980 converted to U.S. dollars at an exchange rate of 1.7050, the rate for 1981, according to *China Statistical Yearbook 2001*, table 17-2, p. 586.

3. Xinhua News Agency, "China's Economy up 9.1% in 2003," January 20, 2004, http://news.xinhuanet.com/english/2004-01/20/content_1285769.htm.

4. Ibid.

5. Xinhua News Agency, "9.1% Surge Epitomizes Sound Growth of Economy," January 20, 2004, http://news.xinhuanet.com/english/2004-01/20/content_1285767.htm.

6. Lu Xueyi, ed., *Dangdai Zhongguo shehui jieceng yanjiu baogao* [Research report on social strata in contemporary China] (Beijing: Shehui kexue wenxian chubanshe [China social sciences publishing house], 2001).

7. Ibid.

8. Economist Intelligence Unit, "Country Briefings: China," http://www.economist.com/countries/china, accessed October 30, 2002.

9. Edward A. Gargan, "A Middle Class Rises in the Cities, Leaving the Masses Behind," *Newsday*, August 4, 2002, p. A05.

10. Liu Haoxing, sociologist, interview by author, September 24, 2002.

11. "Jiang Designates Economic Goals by 2020," *China Daily*, November 10, 2002, p. 1, http://www.cpirc.org.cn.

12. Author's interview with Fan Gang, September 20, 2002.

13. In most locations, migrant workers are not covered by social security in the cities where they work, however.

14. Author's interview with Fan Gang, September 20, 2002.

15. Jeffrey G. Williamson, "Demographic Shocks and Global Factor Flows," in Conference Series no. 46, *Seismic Shifts: The Economic Impact of Demographic Change*, ed. Jane Sneddon Little and Robert K. Triest (Boston: Federal Reserve Bank of Boston, 2001), pp. 247–269; see http://www.bos.frb.org/economic/conf/conf46/conf46h1.pdf.

16. Ibid., p. 251.

17. Bangladesh, China, Hong Kong, India, Indonesia, Japan, Republic of Korea, Malaysia, Myanmar, Nepal, Pakistan, Philippines, Singapore, Sri Lanka, Taiwan, Thailand.

18. Matthew Higgins and Jeffrey G. Williamson, "Age Structure Dynamics in Asia and Dependence on Foreign Capital," *Population and Development Review* 23 (June 1997): pp. 261–293.

19. Ibid., table 3, p. 267.

20. Williamson, "Demographic Shocks and Global Factor Flows," p. 252.

21. Botswana, Cameroon, Gambia, Ghana, Guinea-Bissau, Kenya, Malawi, Mali, Niger, Senegal, Sierra Leone, South Africa, Tanzania, Tunisia, Uganda, Zaire, Zambia, Zimbabwe, Canada, Costa Rica, Dominican Republic, El Salvador, Guatemala, Haiti, Honduras, Jamaica, Mexico, Nicaragua, Trinidad and Tobago, United States, Argentina, Bolivia, Brazil, Chile, Colombia, Ecuador, Guyana, Paraguay, Peru, Uruguay, Venezuela, Bangladesh, China, Hong Kong, India, Indonesia, Israel, Japan, Jordan, South Korea, Malaysia, Pakistan, Philippines, Singapore, Sri Lanka, Syria, Taiwan, Thailand, Austria, Belgium, Denmark, Finland, France, Germany, Greece, Ireland, Italy, Netherlands, Norway, Portugal, Spain, Sweden, Turkey, United Kingdom, Australia, New Zealand, Papua New Guinea.

22. David Bloom and Jeffrey G. Williamson, "Demographic Transitions and Economic Miracles in Emerging Asia," *World Bank Economic Review* 12 (September 1998): 419–455.

23. Williamson, "Demographic Shocks and Global Factor Flows," p. 268.

24. Raymond Foo, Tham Mun Hon, Winner Lee, "Behind the Bamboo Curtain" (Hong Kong: BNP Paribas Peregrine, October 2002).

25. Ibid., p. 73.

26. Paul Krugman, "The Myth of Asia's Miracle, *Foreign Affairs* 78, no. 6 (November/December 1994): 62–78.

27. Alex Frew McMillan, "China Growth Myths Dispelled," CNN Asia, October 29, 2002, from http://archives.cnn.com/2002/BUSINESS/asia/10/29/hk.bnpchina.

28. Anuradha Dayal-Gulati and Aasim M. Husain, "Centripetal Forces in China's Economic Takeoff," *IMF Staff Papers* 49, no. 3 (2002): 364–392, http://www.imf.org/External/Pubs/FT/staffp/2002/03/pdf/gulati.pdf.

29. Ibid., p. 365.

30. Ibid., p. 390.

31. "China to Replace U.S. as the Engine for the World Economy," *People's Daily*, October 2002.

32. Yasheng Huang, *Selling China: Foreign Direct Investment during the Reform Era* (Cambridge: Cambridge University Press, 2003).

33. Ibid., p. 141.

34. "China's Local Trade Barriers: A Hard Nut to Crack," *Transition Newsletter* 12, no. 3 (July–August–September 2001): 11.

35. Gregory C. Chow, *China's Economic Transformation* (Malden, Mass.: Blackwell, 2002).

36. Oliver August, "Chinese Fireworks Could Soon Fizzle Out," *Times* (of London), July 4, 2002, p. 28; http://www.timesonline.co.uk/article/0,,630-346111,00.html.

37. Ibid.

38. Mao Yushi, "The Macroeconomic Implications of Pension Reform in China" (paper presented at China Center for Economic Research/Cato Institute conference, *China's Pension System: Crisis and Challenge,* Beijing, November 8, 2001), p. 3.

39. Li Xiaochao, ed., *China Statistical Yearbook 2001*, table 13-1, p. 401.

40. *China Statistical Yearbook 2002*, table 13-1.

41. Data on GDP by sector attributed to Lu Xueyi, chairman of the Chinese Sociological Association, in "GDP No Longer Sole Index of Growth," *China Business Weekly*, December 16, 2003.

42. Huang, *Selling China*, p. 112.

43. SOE employment dropped from 112.44 million in 1996 to 76.40 million in 2001; data for 1996 from *China Statistical Yearbook 2001*, table 5-1, p. 107, and data for 2001 from *China Statistical Yearbook 2002*, table 5-1.

44. Meredith M. Walker and Richard Alm, "China's Churn" (Dallas: Federal Reserve Bank of Dallas, September 2000), http://www.dallasfed.org/research/pubs/churn.pdf.

45. Ibid., p. 1.

46. *China Statistical Yearbook 2002*, table 13-2.

47. Nelson W. S. Chow, *Socialist Welfare with Chinese Characteristics: The Reform of the Social Security System in China* (Hong Kong: University of Hong Kong, 2000), chap. 2, "Lessons from Socialist Russia and Singapore," and chap. 3, "Social Security as Symbol of Socialist Superiority."

48. Ibid., p. 25. The social insurance regulations introduced in 1951 and 1953 are summarized on pp. 22–25.

49. Ibid., table 13-10. At the exchange rate of 8.27815 in October 2002, 54,772 yuan equaled $6,616.

50. Ibid., table 13-6. At the exchange rate of 8.27815 in October 2002, 75,913 yuan equaled $9,170.

51. Data for August 2004 from People's Bank of China, http://www.pbc.gov.cn/english/diaochatongji/tongjishuju/gofile.asp?file=2004S1.htm. Currency conversion: 17.917 trillion yuan renminbi or $2.960 trillion at exchange rate of 0.120821 on October 16, 2004. Dollars refer to U.S. dollars.

52. OECD, *China in the World Economy*.

53. Pieter Bottelier, "Managing China's Transition Debt: Challenges for Sustained Development," Washington, D.C., mimeo., November 7, 2002, p. 6.

54. Ibid.

55. Ibid., p. 8.

56. Pieter Bottelier, former head of the Beijing office of the World Bank, press conference, Beijing, April 2, 2002.

57. The first IPO, expected in 2005, is likely to be by the Bank of China, which listed its Hong Kong operations as BOC Hong Kong (Holdings) Ltd. in July 2002. The Industrial and Commercial Bank intends to list in Hong Kong, New York, and Singapore in 2006, while the China Construction Bank plans a listing in Hong Kong in 2007, and the Agricultural Bank of China is expected to list sometime after 2008. Each will need to reduce its burden of nonperforming loans to enter the IPO markets and attract foreign partners.

58. Data from People's Bank of China, http://www.pbg.gov.cn.

59. Ibid.

60. Clay Chandler, "Trying to Make Good on Bad-Debt Reform; China Selling Bank Assets to Solve Problem," *Washington Post*, January 15, 2002, p. E-01.

61. Standard & Poor's, *China Banking Outlook 2003–2004* (Beijing: Standard & Poor's, June 2003).

62. "Bank Sector Outlook Stable: S&P," *Shanghai Daily*, September 9, 2003, p. 1.

63. Nicholas R. Lardy, "China's Worsening Debts," *Financial Times*, June 22, 2001, p. 13.

64. John P. Bonin and Yiping Huang, "Foreign Entry into Chinese Banking: Does WTO Membership Threaten Domestic Banks?" (paper presented at City University of Hong Kong conference, "Greater China and the WTO," August 22–24, 2001), p. 23.

65. Ibid.

66. Ibid, p. 24.

67. Standard & Poor's, *China Financial Services Outlook 2004* (Hong Kong: Standard & Poor's, November 2004).

68. Lardy, "China's Worsening Debts," p. 13.

69. Keith Bradsher, "China Announces New Bailout of Big Banks, *New York Times*, January 7, 2004, p. 1.

70. "Bank of China to Get $20 Billion Bailout," *China Daily*, December 26, 2003.

71. The $45 billion was the second capital injection into China's major banks in five years. In 1998 the Ministry of Finance injected 270 billion yuan ($32.5 billion) in capital into the Big Four banks.

72. "China to Write Off $41 Billion Stake in Two Banks," *China Daily*, January 15, 2004.

73. Data from People's Bank of China; data for December 2002 from www.pbc.gov.cn/baogaoyutongjishuju/2002S4.htm. On October 10, 2003, the exchange rate was 0.12108, and 17.917 trillion yuan renminbi equaled $2.164 trillion.

74. Bloomberg.com. "China's GDP Growth Seen Slowing in 2004 as State Curbs Lending," December 23, 2003, at http://quote.blomberg.com/apps/news?pid=10000080&sid=aIO7xeroAP0&refer=asia. Bloomberg report cites an unidentified official as reported in December 2003 in *China's 21st Century Business Herald Newspaper*.

75. *China Statistical Yearbook 2001*, p. 49. At the 1979 exchange rate of 1.56, 417 yuan equal $267.

76. Xinhua News Agency, "9.1% Surge Epitomizes Sound Growth of Economy," January 20, 2004, http://news.xinhuanet.com/english/2004-01/20/content_1285767.htm.

77. Data reported by Nicholas Lardy, Brookings Institution, in comments at "Investing in China's Capital Markets: Where Will WTO-Sparked Reforms Lead?" sponsored by the Asia Society, New York, May 9, 2002.

78. 5 billion yuan represents $604 million at the exchange rate of 8.27815 (October 2002).

79. "PBOC Readjusts Bond Markets," *AsiaPort Daily News*, September 19, 2002, p. 4.

80. Estimate made in January 2004 by Hong Kong actuary Stuart H. Leckie, chairman of the Hong Kong Retirement Schemes Association.

81. Bottelier, "Managing China's Transition Debt," p. 12.

82. Ibid., p. 14.

83. Ibid.

84. Ibid., p. 15.

85. Xinhua News Agency, "24 Million Chinese Urban Residents Need Jobs This Year: Ministry," August 15, 2003.

86. Ibid.

87. Athar Hussain, "Urban Poverty in China: Measurement, Patterns and Policies" (Geneva: International Labor Organization, January 2003), p. 23, http://www.ilo.org/public/english/protection/ses/download/docs/china.pdf.

88. "Jobless Situation to Stay Grave for Years," *China Daily*, November 6, 2003, p. 1.

89. Ibid.

90. Ibid.

91. "China Confronts Grim Job Situation," *China Daily*, April 29, 2002, reposted at http://www.cpirc.org.cn/.

92. China Online, "China's Real Jobless Rate Reaches Warning Level," June 14, 2002, http://www.chinaonline.com.

93. Cai Fang, ed., *2002 nian Zhongguo ren kou yu lao dong wen ti bao gao: cheng xiang jiu ye wen ti yu dui ce* [2002 green book on population and labor: Employment in rural and urban China] (Beijing: She hui ke xue wen xian chu ban she [Chinese Academy of Social Sciences], 2002).

94. "China's Urban Young Jobless up 20%," *China Daily*, June 13, 2002, http://www.cpirc.org.cn.

95. Ibid.

96. Information provided by Zhao Xiaojian, vice minister of labor and social security, quoted in David Murphy, "Nothing More to Lose," *Far Eastern Economic Review*, November 7, 2002, pp. 31–32.

97. Wang Dongjin, vice minister of labor and social security, quoted in Matthew Forney, "Workers' Wasteland," *Time International* 159, no. 12 (June 17, 2002): 40–44.

98. Hu Angang, quoted in Forney, "Worker's Wasteland," pp. 40–44.

99. Comments by Zhang Zuoji, minister of labor and social security (press conference at Sixteenth National Congress of the Communist Party of China, Beijing, November 11, 2002).

100. Ibid.

101. Athar Hussain, "Urban Poverty in China: Measurement, Patterns and Policies," p. 23.

102. Ibid.

103. China Online, "Urban Poverty Not Only Tough to Fight, but also Calculate," April 1, 2002, http://www.chinaonline.com.

104. Ibid.

105. Ibid.

106. In October 2002, 285 yuan equaled $34.42; 435 yuan equaled $52.55.

107. Anders Reutersward, "Labour Market and Social Benefit Policies," in *China in the World Economy*, box 16.1, p. 544.

108. Lu Xueyi, ed., *Dangdai Zhongguo shehui jieceng yanjiu baogao* [Study of class in contemporary Chinese society] (Beijing: China Social Sciences Publishing House, 2001).

109. Ru Xin, Lu Xueyi, and Shan Tianlun, eds., *2001 Shehui lanpishu: zongguo shehui xingshi fengxi yu yuce* [Social blue book 2001: an analysis and forecasting of social conditions in China] (Beijing: Shehui kexue wenxian chubanshe, 2001).

110. Central News Agency, March 7, 2002.

111. Press Conference, Beijing, Sixteenth National Congress of the Communist Party of China, November 11, 2002.

112. Ibid.

113. Robert Holzmann, interview by author, November 27, 2002.

114. Aart Kraay, "Household Saving in China," *World Bank Economic Review,* September 2000, http://www.worldbank.org/research/bios/akraay/Household%20Saving%20in%20China.pdf.

115. Noriyuki Takayama, "Pension Reform of PRC: Incentives, Governance and Policy Options" (paper prepared for the Fifth Anniversary Con-

ference on Challenges and the New Agenda for the People's Republic of China, Asian Development Bank, December 5–6, 2002, Tokyo), p. 16.

116. Ibid.

117. Robert Stowe England, "How Strong Is the Tie Between Aging and Lower Saving?" in *The Macroeconomic Impact of Global Aging: A New Era of Economic Frailty?* (Washington, D.C.: Center for Strategic and International Studies, 2002).

118. Author's interview with Fan Gang, September 20, 2002.

4

China's Social Service Programs

The impact of aging of China will be reflected in concerns about the sustainability of its social security system, paying for health care promises made to the elderly, and the maintenance of savings rates at a level that provides needed funds for investment and government borrowing.[1] In China there is no pay-as-you-go rural social security system and, thus, no worry about sustaining it, although there is concern about how best to set up a funded system to cover the nation's farmers. The urban social security system is still burdened by SOEs despite progress in enlisting non-SOEs to join the system. The urban system suffers from a significant level of underfunding. The challenge for the central government is to reform the system to make it sustainable, to place real funds in the part of the system that is supposed to be funded, and to expand it to include more workers.

China's social security system is limited in scope. It does not cover nonagricultural workers in rural areas, in particular the 130.86 million who work for TVEs, the 11.87 million in rural private enterprises, and the 26.29 million self-employed in 2001. Further, the system does not reach those in rural or urban areas who work in the informal sector—many in the informal sector are migrants, often without official authorization to move from their place of birth to the cities where they can find jobs. China's *hu kou* (personal register) system requires citizens to obtain permission to leave one area of the country to migrate to another. The social security system can grow, however, by increasing participation by businesses to 100 percent, extending coverage to migrant workers, and requiring employers to calculate their contributions against a higher portion of wages.

Programs for Urban Areas

Even without the prospect of rapid aging, China would face a serious challenge in financing its mostly unfunded urban pensions. This is one result of China's move to a market economy. As new businesses arose and expanded and as SOEs cut their workforce, the SOEs were left with a social security burden that was far out of proportion to their ability to sustain it. Employers pay a percentage of their payroll to cover the costs of providing retirement income to retired and laid-off workers. Thus, as the workforce downsized and the number of pensions increased, the flow of funds as a percentage of salary and wages into the social security system was reduced just as the demands for retirement benefits increased. It was primarily the concern about the burden of social security on SOEs that led Chinese authorities to set out to reform the system a decade ago. After some social security reform experiments and after consultation with independent experts, including the World Bank, China adopted sweeping social security reform in 1997.

Urban Pension Reforms of 1997 and 2000

The key change in China's pension reforms occurred in 1995 when the State Council mandated a two-tiered system for social security that would include individual accounts to be funded by both the employer and employee. The reforms were the result of China's leaders concluding that the existing system that provided pensions of 80 percent of average city wages was unsustainable, that future generations should not be burdened with the cost of current workers' pensions, and that the system should move away from pay-as-you-go toward a partly funded system. The broad outline of the reforms China enacted reflected recommendations made to China's leaders by the World Bank. The 1997 reforms made the two-tiered system uniform nationally.

Pensions were set at 20 percent of average city wages for the first tier and with employers and employees contributing 10 percent of salary to individual accounts in the second tier. It was hoped that the establishment of funded accounts to provide an earnings-related pension on top of the basic flat-rate benefit would give China a pension system that would be sustainable during its upcoming period of rapid aging. The benefit from the second tier would be calculated from the amount accumulated in each worker's individual account and not by a defined benefit accrual formula that is typical of pay-as-you-go social security systems.

If the funds in the two-tiered system could be invested to earn a sufficient return, it would help make the system sustainable without imposing the potentially higher contribution burden on employers and employees that a pay-as-you-go system would require. Because the basic pay-as-you-go benefit was greatly reduced for new workers under the pension reform, it is most important that the funds in the individual accounts earn a good rate of return or are credited with a good rate of return to ensure the system provides a final benefit that will be sufficient.[2]

To the extent that the government could reduce the financial burden of providing 80 percent pensions, it would then have funds to distribute to the unemployed, the abjectly poor, and the elderly without family support. Such support could help address public concerns about the growing income gap, unemployment, and corruption that have fanned public discontent and social unrest. Economics professor Mao Yushi captures this understanding of reform when he suggests that "the key problem of pension reform is not to increase national savings, but how to help poor people."[3]

Under the reforms enacted by the State Council in 1997, China's pension system continued its transition away from the concept of a pure pay-as-you-go system with a defined benefit based on about 80 percent of the average salary of workers. The new system the central government created that year has three tiers: a basic benefit based on 20 percent of the city's average wage; a defined contribution benefit based on employer and employee contributions into individual accounts; and voluntary employer-sponsored supplementary pensions, including what is known in China as enterprise annuity plans. The largest piece of this three-tiered system is the individual account.

The new system was designed to reduce the burden of social security on SOEs. Under the reform, SOEs pool their contributions, first at the local level and later at the provincial level, so that local or provincial social security bureaus pay out the benefits. This was designed to help ensure that retired workers receive pension payments in a timely manner. Before the reforms, SOEs paid pensions from their own funds, and some SOEs found it increasingly difficult to afford the pensions because they had a shrinking number of active workers contributing into the system. Some fell behind on payments. As a result, many retirees were not receiving pension payments on a regular basis.

After the economy began to shift workers out of the SOE system, China's State Council adopted a policy that requires all urban employers, including non-SOEs, to participate in the social security system.[4] Many non-SOEs do not wish to participate in the system because the contribution costs (charges against payroll) are high and not in line with the benefits that the company's workforce will ultimately reap from the system. The non-SOEs tend to interpret the cost of joining as a form of tax. The high contribution rates are designed to meet the cost of benefits to retirees from the SOEs and the growing army of laid-off workers. With public cajoling and the use of various threats and penalties, provincial and other local authorities have been able to get more of the non-SOEs to join.

The newly redesigned social system was not a detailed blueprint; it was a general outline. It left a lot of unfinished business, loose ends, loopholes, and daunting tasks to be resolved in the future. The implementation of the reforms varies widely across provinces. Its detailed provisions, such as how to calculate the rate of return on the funds in the second tier accounts, are sometimes regarded by local authorities as guidelines, not mandates. Local and provincial authorities also have to find ways to enlist the participation of all the collectives and private sector firms that were not previously part of the system.

The cost of the pension reform in its current design is a huge burden on all enterprises and their workers. Tier 1 was to be financed by the employer's contributions of 30 percent; this contribution was to provide a basic 20 percent benefit at retirement.

The individual accounts of tier 2 are funded by a combined 11 percent contribution rate from the employer and the worker. The worker's contribution began at 4 percent and is gradually rising to 8 percent by 2005, while the employer's contribution to the individual accounts began at 7 percent and is gradually declining to 3 percent. The defined contribution system or tier 2 pays the retiree a monthly pension of 1/120 of the balance in the account at retirement. If the worker contributes into the system for 35 years and the rate of return is the same as for the growth of wages, the second tier is designed to provide a pension equal to 38.5 percent of the worker's former wage.[5]

Despite successes in persuading business to join the urban social security system, the proportion of covered workers is rather low. At the end of 2000, it was estimated that about 106 million workers and another 34 million retirees were covered by it (table 4.1).[6] At first glance it looks as if only 45.8 percent (106 million) of the 231.51 million urban workforce was included in the urban social security system in 2000.[7] However, the total urban workforce includes 81.63 million whose work units are not identified; many, perhaps most, of these workers are civil servants in the government sector at one level or another who are covered by a separate pension system, or they are members of the 2.5 million People's Liberation Army and other affiliated police forces.[8] Jobs of the others among the 81.63 million workers in this group are unknown. Subtracting the group of workers whose employer organizations do not appear eligible to join the urban social security system leaves a potential group of 149.88 million eligible workers. Within that subgroup, the 106 million participants represent a coverage rate of 70.7 percent of the potential participants. And, if the 21.36 million self-employed are subtracted, what remains is 128.52 million workers and a coverage rate of 82.5 percent, although the self-employed are supposed to participate in the system. It would appear that there is *not* a lot of room for further extending the urban social security system in the formal sector without expanding it to the businesses in the rural sector.

Declining Role for SOEs

In China in the past, workers at SOEs received low wages but typically received generous pensions equal to 80 percent or more of their wages; in addition, they received health care, housing subsidies, unemployment pay, and other benefits. Many in the workforce before the introduction of social security reform in 1997 are still eligible for the old generous pensions and most other ben-

Table 4.1. Basic Old-Age Pensions for Workers of Enterprises
in Cities and Towns

	1997	1998	1999	2000	2001	2002
Number of participants at year end (in millions)	112	112	125	135	140	149
Workers	87	85	95	104	106	113
Retirees	25	27	30	31	34	36
Income (billion yuan RMB)	134	113	197	228	243	317
Expenditures (billion yuan RMB)	125	151	192	212	232	284
Accumulated surplus (billion yuan RMB)	68	59	73	95	105	161

Sources: *China Labor Statistical Yearbook 2003*, table 11.28, p. 556, and table 11.29, p. 558.

efits. Workers are now divided into three categories: the "old men" who retired before 1997, the "middle men" working in 1997 who would get the new benefits with a minimum transition guarantee, and the "new men" who joined the workforce after 1997 and who get the new benefits.

Just as the need to reduce medical costs at SOEs has driven health reform in China (see the section on health care in this chapter), so too has that same need been a primary driver of social security reform, especially the sweeping reform adopted by the State Council in 1997 and amended in 2000.[9] The social security reforms transformed the urban social security system from a simple pay-as-you-go plan, with benefits up to 80 percent of salary, to a three-tiered pension system. The three tiers comprise a basic pay-as-you-go tier that pays out a benefit equal to 20 percent of the worker's wages; a second tier of individual accounts that was designed to accumulate enough funds over a career to pay a benefit equal to 38.5 percent of the average worker's wages; and a third tier of voluntary supplementary enterprise pensions that would be financed by contributions at levels that workers determine personally. Together, the system's three tiers were designed to eventually allow for the creation of a retirement benefit close to the 80 percent of salary that was provided under the former system.

While the reform of the urban pension system has been a focus of the central government, it is important to put the size of the urban pension system in context of the larger population. The urban population in 2000 was only 37 percent of China's total population, about 458.8 million people.[10] By contrast 63 percent China's population—783.8 million—are classified as rural, even though many of them live in villages that are fairly large and might be deemed urban in the West.[11] The number of workers in the urban workforce totaled 247.8 million in 2002,[12] but only 113 million worked for enterprises that were part of the urban social security system (figure 4.1).[13] Of the 247.8 million urban workers, 71.6 million worked for SOEs, 11.2 million worked for urban collective enterprises (UCEs, which operate as subunits of SOEs), 20 million worked for private enterprises, 7.6 million worked for FIEs, and another 22.7 million were self-employed (often with small businesses with a few employees) (see table 3.4).

Non-SOEs have been reluctant to participate in the social security system because contributions entail a significant new labor cost, which varies from location to location but can approach 30 percent or more of payroll. Non-SOEs include millions of small family farms, which are businesses operated on land owned by local governments but assigned for use by small family farms. Rural areas also contain a huge base of nonagricultural enterprises that are collectively owned by towns and villages. These TVEs have been one of the most powerful engines of China's economic growth since the early 1980s, when reform efforts began to take hold. The government targeted rural areas for these mostly light manufacturers of consumer goods so they could absorb the exodus of millions of surplus workers from farms. Most of the TVEs, which can be owned collectively or by local governments or local communities, have been established in the coastal and southern areas of China and not in the interior provinces, resulting in a growing disparity in income and wealth between the coast and the interior.

The TVE engine contributed the largest share to the nation's economic growth from the mid-1980s to the mid-1990s. Their gains were propelled by their exemption from central planning

Figure 4.1. Employment in Selected Urban Enterprise by Type

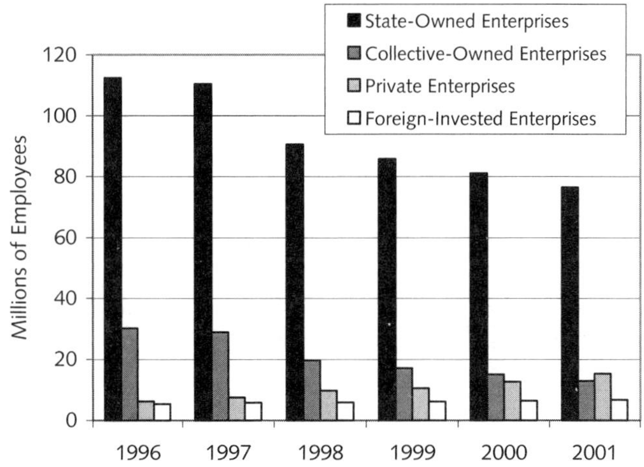

Source: *China Statistical Yearbook* 2001, 2002, table 5-1, p. 107.

directives of the state and their exposure to market disciplines. Employment growth in this sector peaked in 1996, at which point TVEs employed 135 million or 27.5 percent of the rural workforce.[14] Although their work might have been seasonal or part-time, at that point there were more workers in TVEs in the rural areas than there were at SOEs in the urban areas, which employed 112.44 million. The location of these businesses in rural areas has transformed the earnings profile of China's rural residents, with 47 percent of their income now coming from the nonagricultural sector.[15] By contrast, in 1985 only 26 percent of income in the rural areas was nonagricultural.[16]

After peaking in 1996 at 135 million, employment by TVEs declined by almost 10 million over the next two years, falling to 125 million in 1997. Since 1998, employment has been rising slowly, but steadily, hitting nearly 133 million in 2002.[17] Meanwhile, the growth of employment by private enterprises in rural areas nearly tripled, from 5.5 million in 1996 to 14.1 million in 2002,[18] creating more new jobs than the TVEs had lost. While the TVE engine was not creating jobs at the clip it had before 1998, after 1995 profits continued to grow, albeit at a slower pace, rising from 219 billion yuan in 1996 to 339 billion yuan in 2000.[19] Despite the ups and downs in employment, the TVE sector has grown steadily in revenues and profits ever since the mid-1990s.

In the coming decade an estimated 70 million rural Chinese are expected to exit farming and migrate across the countryside, possibly to live and work illegally in the urban areas, particularly in the coastal areas, according to economic simulations by the OECD.[20] By 1999, this exit from the farms had already created an estimated 100 million unregistered workers, or "floating population," who had taken up jobs in the cities in what economists call the informal sector or shadow economy. The Population Reference Bureau has estimated China's floating population at 130 million.[21]

The non-SOE sector also includes UCEs that, like the TVEs, were free from centrally planned directives and more exposed to market discipline. They operate as subunits of SOEs and are subject indirectly to government direction and control. Together the rural and urban collectives now produce a larger share of industrial output than the SOEs, although since 1996 the UCEs have steadily lost employees, falling from 30.2 million workers in 1996 to 11.2 million in 2002, in tandem with the decline of the SOE sector. A third group of businesses includes privately held businesses (in both urban and rural areas), shareholding enterprises, joint ownership enterprises, and foreign-owned units (see table 3.4).

China's strong economic growth in recent years and its increasingly competitive markets have led to a fair amount of optimism among some observers about China's ability to handle its social problems. Economist Qu Hongbin of HSBC Bank in Hong Kong estimates that 27 million of China's 71.6 million workers in SOEs will lose their jobs over the next five years.[22] Yet, annual average government tax and other revenues of $250 billion a year and more will be sufficient to fund a social safety net for them and other workers who may be unemployed as a result of increased competition generated from China's membership in the WTO, according to economist Andy Xie at Morgan Stanley in Hong Kong.[23]

Chinese officials have been touting how much the government is spending on social welfare benefits. In October 2002 former labor minister Zhang reported that the central government had, over the previous four years, spent 84.7 billion yuan[24] on living allowances for laid-off workers who had reported to reemployment centers.[25] The centers have also helped workers receive their pensions. China's social unemployment system, set up in

1993, covered 140 million workers by the end of 2001[26] and has remained in surplus (table 4.1).

Social spending of all types by the central government has been increasing dramatically, rising from 1 percent in 1997 to 6.3 percent of the entire national budget in 2001, according to Minister of Finance Xiang Huaicheng.[27] In his annual report in March 2002,[28] Xiang reported that in 2001 Beijing allocated 98.2 billion yuan for various social welfare measures: this included 34.9 billion yuan ($4.22 billion) to subsidize the old-age insurance fund and 31 billion yuan ($3.74 billion) to replenish the national social security trust fund. In addition, social spending included 13.6 billion yuan for basic living allowances for workers laid off from SOEs, 2.3 billion yuan for subsistence allowances for poor urban residents, and 8.4 billion yuan for disabled military service members and their families and for other social welfare and relief funds.[29] Benefits from social welfare spending were distributed to 47 million people.[30]

The challenge for Chinese authorities will be not simply to come up with funds for a social safety net. Ultimately workers want jobs that can sustain them with a living wage and health and retirement benefits. At present, the private sector and many FIEs are not providing the kinds of benefits, or anything close to those benefits, that workers routinely enjoyed at SOEs.

Underfunding of Pensions

The urban social security system, which in 2000 covered 106 million of the 212.7 million urban workers in the formal sector,[31] has large unfunded future liabilities, initially officially estimated at about 22.5 percent of gross domestic product (GDP) for 1995.[32] Independent estimates run higher. The World Bank has variously estimated the amount at 94 percent of GDP in 2000 and 71 percent of GDP in 2001.[33] An actuarial analysis, completed in 2000 by Aetna Insurance (now part of ING) in cooperation with the MLSS, found a potential shortfall of 145 percent of GDP.[34] Some of the discrepancies in the estimates arise from different methods of calculating the liabilities. The Aetna estimate of the shortfall is higher, for example, because it uses the actual patterns of retirement—which reflect a strong trend toward early retirement—instead of official retirement ages to determine when workers leave employment and begin to receive a benefit. The pattern of retirement used in the Aetna study is based on relatively complete actuarial data available from the city of Nanjing.

The rise in layoffs has been a key factor in pushing up the level of underfunding in the urban pension plan system and in straining the pension reform that had been enacted to take a great degree of the pressure off the SOEs. The reform was designed to do this by pooling all pension contributions into a single pool at the provincial level in support of the individual accounts. The reform also made it possible for SOEs to pay contributions on the basis of their current payroll, independent of their legacy pension liabilities. The reform provided for a local social security bureau to pool and oversee the cash flow from various enterprises as well as pay benefits. This approach was to ensure that retirees received their benefits instead of relying on enterprises that were hard-pressed to meet their payrolls, let alone pay pensions.

Except in six provinces—four of them the municipal provinces of Beijing, Chongqing, Shanghai, and Tianjin as well as the provinces of Liaoning and Hainan—authorities have not been able to implement the province-wide pools of assets that were envisioned in the original reform.[35] Twenty-four provinces have not achieved province-wide pooling. (China counts Taiwan as its 31st province, but Taiwan has a separate pension system.) In the 24 provinces, pooling has occurred at the local or regional level, which leaves China with a highly fragmented pension system.

The new pension system started out with fairly narrow coverage concentrated on SOEs. At the end of 1998, for example, coverage comprised 78.4 percent of workers in SOEs, 16.2 percent of workers in collective enterprises (both urban and rural), and 5 percent of workers in other urban enterprises (those in the private sector.)[36] Coverage has expanded well beyond that core in some provinces—Shanghai, for example—where authorities ensure that FIEs and some private enterprises participate fully in the system, sometimes under threat of regulatory retaliation. Economist Hu Feng Yun, former deputy director of the Shanghai Bureau of Social Security, has stated that "the government took strong measures to force them [non-SOEs] to participate."[37] Strong measures included threatening to deny or withdraw necessary permits to do business as well as stiff fines and penalties, Hu explained.

Estimates of the level of underfunding in the urban social security system vary widely and, as a whole, have been rising over time. The Chinese government has pegged the shortfall between

$122 billion and $244 billion. In 2001 Standard & Poor's calculated the unfunded liability at $200 billion.[38] The Bank of China International has estimated the shortfall at $850 billion. Some estimates in the private sector have topped $1 trillion.

In 2000, Yan Wang et al. did a series of computer simulations and an equilibrium analysis of the shortfall in China's pension system for the World Bank.[39] The simulation assumes that life expectancy rises from 70.3 years to 76.9 years in 2050 and that the total fertility rate rises from 1.9 to 2.1. The projection assumes that the workforce will stop growing sometime between 2015 and 2020 and decline afterward. The old-age dependency ratio will rise steadily from 11 percent to 25 percent in 2030 and 36 percent in 2050.[40] The World Bank estimated the urban system's implicit pension debt (IPD)—the present value of the unfunded liability that would exist if the pension system were frozen—to be 71 percent of GDP in 2000. That would have placed it that year at 6.328 trillion yuan ($873 billion). The study relies on prior work done by Dorfman and Sin in a paper that was not made public.[41]

The World Bank's baseline scenario (the current system without changes) is that over the next 50 years the implicit pension debt would be constantly rising in absolute value but declining as a percentage of GDP. In 2050, after many of those in the old, generous system die, the implicit pension debt would still be at 33.1 percent of GDP, or about 37.139 trillion yuan ($11.7 trillion).[42] By 2050 the accumulated net deficit would be 10.273 trillion ($1.24 trillion). These numbers suggest that the current system is unsustainable without further reforms.

Paying for its social security promises is going to become increasingly costly for China's government. The World Bank[43] found annual deficits within the urban pension system rising from an estimated 6 billion yuan in 2002 to 68 billion yuan in 2005 and 115 billion yuan in 2010.[44] These numbers now look low. The national government's 2002 budget for its social security subsidy, half of which is earmarked for pension benefits, was already topping 41 billion yuan ($10 billion). On the basis of this spending level, Leckie estimates that the annual deficit was already around 40 billion yuan in 2002.[45]

In recent years the national government has begun to subsidize some of the previous shortfall in an effort to see to it that retirees are getting their pensions. Labor unrest has occurred numerous times in the wake of mass layoffs, especially when workers were unable to get either their pensions or unemployment pay. As noted earlier, in 2001 Finance Minister Xiang Huaicheng reported that Beijing allocated 34.9 billion yuan to subsidize old-age pension payments[46] and 31 billion yuan to replenish the National Social Security Fund,[47] which Beijing set up in 2000 in order to help subsidize the social security system in areas that were having trouble making pension payments as well as to provide social payments to the poor and unemployed.

The national government has been able to sell off some of its shares in SOEs to raise money to inject into the National Social Security Fund. In April 2002 the government's SOE share was estimated to be worth $387 billion,[48] or about two-thirds of the stock market's total capitalization at that time. The government first tried to sell shares on the stock exchanges in June 2001 and January 2002, and each time the action led to across-the-board declines in the value of shares. When Beijing announced in June 2002 that it would suspend share sales for domestic initial public offerings (IPOs) and rights (but not international), the stock markets revived temporarily. This was seen first as a retreat on pension reform. Beijing then announced, however, that it would sell portions of SOEs privately to foreign investors and, in November 2002, issued new rules allowing the sale by public tender of nontradable stakes in listed firms held by the government,[49] ending a ban on such sales that had been in place since 1995. The new rules still do not allow foreign investors or firms to take majority stakes in banks, insurers, telecommunication companies, retailers, auto manufacturers, and energy companies. This new approach to selling off portions of SOEs could lead to new injections of capital into the National Social Security Fund, which in November 2003 held 133 billion yuan ($16 billion)[50] in assets.

Empty Individual Accounts

Rising levels of pension payments have, in effect, sabotaged one of social security reform's goals—the creation of individual accounts into which employers and employees can put funds toward their retirement. For now, however, funding the accounts remains controversial until the central government concludes that its experiment in funding those accounts in Liaoning Province have been a success. (See discussion below on Liaoning.) The individual-accounts provision has the potential to transform China's pay-as-you-go pension system into one that is predominantly prefunded—a transformation that would, over time, clearly increase the aggregate level of pension assets if the system were to attract most of China's urban workers. In many parts of the country, however, local authorities in charge of these accounts have used the funds in the accounts to pay for benefits to workers, leaving the accounts empty or purely notional. The level of funds required to make the accounts fully funded was 14 billion yuan ($1.69 billion) in 1997, rising to 45 billion yuan ($5.44 billion) in 1998, 100 billion yuan ($12.08 billion) in 1999, and 199 billion yuan ($24.04 billion) in 2000.[51]

As their ancestors did before them, many Chinese workers must save for their own retirement without the benefit of tax deductions or tax-free gains within a retirement account. Until recently, the only way to save was to deposit money in bank accounts, where it earns a modest rate of return, usually 1.9 percent (price inflation is approximately 0.7 percent). Life insurance companies offer individual life insurance/savings policies, but without any tax advantages. Nevertheless, some Chinese workers have chosen to buy such plans, driving up the life insurance companies' premium income, which rose from about 30 yuan per capita in 1996 to 100 yuan per capita in 2000.[52] This has boosted the size of China's relatively small life insurance industry, which traces its modern roots back only to the beginning of the reform era in 1978 when the central government allowed the re-creation of state-owned insurance companies. So-called commercial insurance (as opposed to social insurance by the government) was not allowed before 1978.

The questions of when and how these accounts will be funded led professors Qixiang Sun of Beijing University and John W. Maxwell of Indiana University to look for reasons why a high payroll contribution rate of 24 percent (and often higher) could not sustain China's pension system. They found that the system is not working because widespread evasion of the contributions is practiced by businesses that are part of the system. Sun and Maxwell calculated that the level of evasion is a hefty 50 percent. Beijing University economist Yaohui Zhao[53] points out that collections of contributions often fall short because pension administration agencies lack effective collection instruments and even the incentive to enforce the collection.[54] At the other end of the arrangement, individuals and businesses also lack incentives to participate and make full contributions.

The State Council's design of the individual account system is structured to gradually increase the amount of money employees pay into the system and gradually decrease the amount employers pay over time. The initial arrangement for funding the accounts assigns a 7 percent of payroll contribution to be paid by the employer and 4 percent paid by employees for a total 11 percent of wages. Gradually, with annual increments, the employee's portion of the contribution is raised to 8 percent, leaving 3 percent for the employer. As employees pay contributions into the accounts and learn that they are empty, they increasingly view their contribution as a "tax" and not a contribution. As this funding transition occurs, the relative costs on labor remain the same, but employees see more being taken out of their paycheck to go into accounts. The right of workers to the amounts in their accounts is not protected by law.

Urban Areas—A Pilot Project

In 2000, Chinese authorities, concerned about the full implementation of the urban pension system, devised a pilot program to be tested in the northeastern coastal province of Liaoning in the southern area of a region of China known to many outsiders as Manchuria. Liaoning's provincial capital, Shenyang, was the secondary capital of China for 350 years during the Qing dynasty that fell in 1911. Many SOEs engaged in heavy industry and high technology are based in Liaoning.

The pilot program was devised to address several perceived problems that delayed pooling in most provinces and left individual accounts empty. The experimental Liaoning pension system uses unique methods of calculating the benefit for the first tier and funding individual accounts in the second tier of the system. The redesign provides workers with a larger basic benefit and a reduced individual account to be funded. The rebalancing of the first two tiers represents a more optimum design for social security, according to Mu Huaizhong, a Liaoning University economics professor who has studied social security systems around the world.[55] Mu believes the reform better serves the need to keep the enterprises competitive while it provides a more secure retirement.

The design of the Liaoning pilot project raised the level of the basic pay-as-you-go tier from 20 percent to 30 percent of city average wages. To pay for this, employers had to raise their contribution for the basic pension from 13 percent to 20 percent of wages. Also, the second tier will support a lower final pension benefit (down from 38.5 percent to 28 percent). Contributions into the individual accounts—now entirely paid from each worker's wages—are reduced from 11 percent to 8 percent. Investment of the funded accounts was transferred to the social security agency at the provincial level.

Under previous guidelines, the real funds in the individual accounts were managed as a single pool, and the investments were initially limited to bank savings deposits. Zhang Xiao Long, an economist, reports that by July 1, 2002, individual accounts in Liaoning totaled 2.92 billion yuan ($352 million),[56] representing one full year of contributions at 8 percent of wages from 4.73 million workers in the urban pension system.[57] Every six months, individual workers are provided statements informing them of the funds in their accounts, Zhang says.[58]

The full funding of the individual accounts funds for the period beginning July 1, 2001, does not make up for prior shortfalls. Further, at the same time that the Liaoning social insurance bureau started to fund the individual accounts, the central government was sending a sizable subsidy to pay for the basic pension benefit of retired workers. Thus, continued diversion of money earmarked for individual accounts was unnecessary. The province hired a consultant, Hewitt Associates, to recommend how to invest its assets, but Hewitt has not publicly reported the findings. Suggestions include possible investment in bonds for the construction of a hydroelectric dam.

In July 2004, Liaoning entered the fourth year of full funding of individual accounts although the public seems to have paid scant attention to the accumulated sums in individual accounts and in total earnings in these accounts. For the first year, ending June 30, 2002, authorities declared the accounts had earned 1.88 percent, even though the actual returns on the funds were lower. The mayor of Shenyang, Chen Zhenggao, has publicly reported that 1.37 million urban workers in his city had joined the social security system by the end of 2002 and had contributed 2.38 billion yuan ($286.7 million) to the program for the entire year.[59]

Liaoning and two other northeast provinces—Heilongjiang and Jilin—have been a key concern of the central government. The concern arises from the higher-than-average concentration of SOEs in this region, which has produced a high level of unemployment and social unrest. The unemployment rate for Shenyang, calculated with the method used by Athar Hussain, could be as high as 17 percent.

In Liaoning Province, for example, major labor unrest occurred in the wake of massive layoffs, including 515,000 in 2001 and another 500,000 in 2002, from SOEs.[60] In March 2002 Liaoning Province experienced labor unrest after mass layoffs from Liaoyang's bankrupt Ferroalloy Factory and Daqing's giant PetroChina facility. Tens of thousands of workers gathered for one of the largest public demonstrations in more than a decade. China responded with a mixed policy of rewards and punishments. Some labor activists were arrested. To quell the unrest, authorities raised the level of benefits provided to the laidoff workers, many of whom were in their 40s. The lump sums paid in these settlements severed the link between the workers and the enterprise, making the workers ineligible for any retirement benefit.

Han Dongfang, a Hong Kong labor activist, warns that while the workers in Daqing and Liaoyang "took what they could get," workers view it as an incomplete settlement of what they are owed by their employer and the government.[61] The workers have not relinquished their claims for full compensation, he adds. Han, who has a radio show on Radio Free Asia and publishes the *China Labour Bulletin*[62] from Hong Kong, has frequently reported on workers he has interviewed inside China who have been active in providing information on labor protests and demonstrations. He provided important, and often exclusive, reporting on labor protests in Daqing and Laoying in the spring of 2002.

It is difficult to assess the potential of adopting and implementing the Liaoning pilot program in all the other provinces. Yaohui Zhao and Jianguo Xu suggest that the Liaoning pilot reform, on the whole, offers more disincentive than the old system for attracting nonparticipating enterprises.[63] Yet, Mayor Chen's report says that participation by enterprises is so high that the program has enrolled 97 percent of the eligible workforce. The social insurance program was also able to meet its obligations to pay pensions to 582,000 retirees, he said. (As noted earlier, however, self-employed workers are probably not part of the system, and employers may have greatly reduced their contributions to the system through negotiation with local authorities.)

The ability of Liaoning to continue to fund the individual accounts, coupled with reports from Shenyang about the ability of the program to meet pension obligations to retirees, strengthens the supporters who want to see the plan adopted elsewhere. However, the fact that the central government also subsidized the program in an amount similar to the level of the funds that went into the individual accounts suggests that it might be expensive to expand it to all the provinces, especially those with high levels of unemployment from closure of SOEs. China's rising wealth should, however, make it easier for the country to afford expanding the program to such provinces as Heilongjiang and Jilin and to other provinces where unemployment and labor unrest pose a significant problem. In fact, Premier Wen Jiabao has vowed to revitalize the three northeastern provinces—Liaoning, Heilongjiang, and Jilin—with investments in new technology and readjustment of their economic structure.[64] This could conceivably include reforming social security in the two provinces along the lines of the Liaoning pilot reform program.

Programs for Rural Areas

The State Council introduced old-age insurance schemes for rural residents in 1991, and they were placed under the management of the Ministry of Civil Affairs. The schemes did not pay very much, were sometimes seen by the rural population to be a tax, and therefore did not generate widespread support. In 1998 these schemes were transferred to the Ministry of Labor and Social Security (MLSS).

So far, the rural insurance program has enrolled only about 2.8 percent of the rural population.[65] Only half those who participated paid in enough to receive a monthly payment of 50 yuan ($6.04).[66] China also supports a rural social relief program for the indigent elderly who have no dependents, are not able-bodied, and have no money (known as the three noes). This program paid only about 57 yuan ($6.89) per month in 1996.[67] There is no government-sponsored retiree health care in rural areas. Working-age peasants have to pay their own medical expenses, and rural facilities and doctors are sparse. Rural China's oft-praised system of "barefoot doctors" and rural clinics has disintegrated over the past decade.[68]

There are currently few major proposals from the government to aid the rural elderly, a problem that presumably could be alleviated in the long term with a further relaxation of one-child policy. The task of incorporating rural populations into a national social security system is daunting in view of the difficulties and disincentives in both the current system and many proposed reforms. The government has begun to build and is planning to build more collective care centers for the elderly, but plans are modest in view of the potential problem of caring for hundreds of millions of rural elderly.

Little thought has been given to assistance for rural areas. Few suggest that the rural areas be integrated into a national social security system, which, while desirable, appears to be infeasible at this time, according to Pieter Bottelier, who headed the World Bank's Beijing office from 1993 to 1997.[69] Meanwhile, a voluntary pension savings scheme introduced in the mid-1990s has attracted only 60 million participants, with only 1.08 million now collecting pension benefits.[70] Authorities hope to propose a new social security system—designed jointly by the Department of Rural Social Security under the MLSS and the Center for Employment and Social Security Studies at Tsinghua University—that would be available to farmers throughout China.

Bottelier suggests that the government might do more to strengthen the security of rural dwellers by strengthening the land rights of rural migrants so they have "something to fall back on in the event urban employment does not work out."[71] Bottelier also recommends that rural migrants be given a temporary *hu kou*, on a experimental basis in some provinces, so they can be integrated into the urban social security system.

Qiao urges the construction of more elderly care nursing homes or day care centers in rural areas and also recommends that local governments provide basic welfare support for the elderly who do not have personal or family resources.[72] Qiao further suggests strengthening community support in both cities and rural areas. He recommends an official, separate social security system for rural areas instead of ad hoc reliance on bank savings by rural dwellers. Qiao also urges Chinese authorities to encourage daughters—to whom society has not traditionally assigned the care of parents—to support and care for their elderly parents. Daughters could, of course, voluntarily assume that responsibility, Qiao says.

Health Care

As China transforms its command economy to a market economy, medical care is becoming more costly for workers and retirees, and fewer workers have the high level of health benefits that once prevailed in the state-owned enterprise sector. The rural population's health care system has moved toward a more market-based system and away from the past, when the government provided minimal basic services at a low cost or for free. The quality of medical care has greatly advanced in rural areas; but, because patients must pay most of the cost of the services and many are poor farmers, part-time workers, or work at firms without health benefits, they often forgo basic health services.

In urban areas, although the quality of medical care has advanced greatly, enterprises are taking steps to change their health care system to reduce their costs and put more of the burden on employees. Non-SOEs are less likely to have the generous health benefits of the state-owned sector. At the same time, the state-owned enterprise sector is shrinking, which means that the portion of workers who can look forward to retiree health care protections is also shrinking.

Efforts to contain the costs of SOE health care programs began in the late 1980s after SOEs were required to make a profit. At that time firms began to set ceilings on the amount of medical expenses they would pay for each worker. Some firms set up funds for medical care for workers, who would use the funds when they became ill. Beginning in the mid-1990s, several areas of the country experimented with a number of pilot projects to control health care expenses. The cities of Jiujiang and Zhengjiang embarked on the "three rivers project," inspired by Medisave schemes in

Singapore, which succeeded in expanding the number of work-ers covered—the cost of coverage cost employers less so they could afford to join—as well as reducing the overall health care costs for SOEs.

In 1996 the State Council decided to expand this program throughout China.[73] By 2003, the Jiujiang-Zhengjiang approach had been expanded to 50 cities. Chow agrees the plans may have been successful in cutting costs but questions the haste of the State Council's decision to extend the programs without first learning whether the health of workers was adversely affected.[74] These programs require employers or employees to set aside a portion of their annual income in individual medical savings accounts. If workers use up all the funds in their accounts, they can then be reimbursed from a social-pooling fund, which limits how much it pays, sometimes covering only 40 percent of the costs from the social-pooling scheme.

In a study of the effectiveness of the health care reform efforts in China, including a pilot project in Zhengjiang and Jiujiang, Gordon G. Liu et al. find that this approach reduces costs in the short run and is more equitable in that more enterprises are will-ing to provide the service. They conclude "there [are] not enough solid financial resources to ensure the entire urban China health services through the new insurance program, particularly in those remote and economically poor regions."[75] This will leave a large portion of the population unable to afford the health care they need.

Throughout China, but especially in rural areas, tuberculosis and hepatitis are persistent risks and an aging population is espe-cially vulnerable. In the rural areas, the rates of these diseases are higher and the poor elderly usually cannot afford available pre-ventive treatments. A World Bank–funded effort to promote diag-nosis and treatment of tuberculosis in China found that, although a free diagnosis encouraged people to visit local hospitals for tests, hospitals were not referring them to dispensaries for treatment.[76] Bates Gill et al. also contend that the inability of many in China to receive adequate health care enhances the potential for outbreaks of diseases such as AIDS.[77] And, both rural and urban poor, in-cluding the elderly, are falling between the cracks of China's emerging safety net.[78]

Chinese authorities do, however, point to some encouraging indicators: the number of doctors per 1,000 residents rose from 1.58 in 1990 to 2.28 in 2000.[79] Other indicators are moving in the opposite direction, however: the number of hospital beds declined from 3.49 per 1,000 in 1990 to 2.11 per 1,000 in 2000.

Improvements in the infant mortality rate—an overall indicator of a nation's health—have been quite modest during the past two decades. Infant mortality was 35 per 1,000 in 1981 and fell only slightly to 32 in 2000, according to the United Nations Children's Fund.[80] This lack of significant improvement since the reform era began contrasts with the steady improvement compared with the pre-1949 period, when infant mortality was at 200 per 1,000. Infant mortality declined to 193 per 1,000 in 1954 and, further, to 81 per 1,000 in 1958.

While changes in China's health care system have reduced costs to local governments in rural areas and SOEs in urban areas, those who become ill have to personally pay an increasing portion of the cost of treating their illness, no matter how poor they are. The China National Heath Services Surveys report that out-of-pocket expenses for those who became ill increased more than 60 percent between the 1992 and 1997, rising from 28 percent to 44 percent of the cost of services. The number of people who did not seek care when they were ill rose from 41 percent to 50 percent.[81]

Social Service Programs Vulnerable to Demographic Change

China has chosen a slow, step-by-step strategy to pension reform and to its larger economic restructuring as well. China, however, cannot grow its way out of its aging problem without significantly advancing reforms, including steps to reduce the high payroll costs that act as a disincentive for non-SOEs to join the system.[82] Reforms will require a sizable contribution rate by the employer, approximately 19 to 20 percent (no contributions are made on wages that are above three times the area's average wage). This makes it difficult for the system to attract significant full participation by enterprises beyond the SOEs. Indeed, some observers conclude that China's pension reform is flawed precisely because during its evolution the aim was not to create an optimal social security system but was to help restructure of the SOE sector instead.

Zhao and Xu note that the pension reforms of 1997 and 2000 removed the SOE's ultimate and sole responsibility for funding growing pension liabilities—one of the stumbling blocks to hard budget constraints on SOEs—and, thus, helped bring greater discipline to their management.[83] However, the reform has not yet succeeded in overcoming the system's financial imbalances. Zhao and Xu importantly contend that the reforms do not sufficiently respond the long-term challenge of aging and suggest that the best way for young workers to be assured of a safe retirement is to start saving for it themselves through mandatory payroll-funded accounts.

A debate is likely over further reforms to reshape and adjust the current pension system to make it sustainable during the upcoming period of rapid aging. Consensus exists about the assumption that the best way to move pension reform forward is to have the state assume some or even all of the unfunded liabilities of the current system in all its variations while new reforms to lower payroll contribution rates are designed. Beyond that, most advocates for further reform want a system that can be expanded to additional workers, including rural workers in TVEs, so that more of the working-age population will have a secure retirement income. Zhao and Xu call for a radical next step: a completely prefunded plan with no pay-as-you-go tier but with a basic benefit guarantee, an option that many observers believe is not realistic for China. Zhao and Xu calculate that, if the full range of urban and rural businesses are drawn into this system, the payroll tax would have to be only 15.8 percent—with 5.6 percent funding current and future retirees in the old system and 10.2 percent funding individual accounts.

A World Bank study by Wang Yan et al.[84] suggests that extending the current system to more enterprises without further reform would leave it vulnerable to aging. Initially, however, expanding the coverage of the current system to all formal sectors in the urban area would work to improve financial condition of the system between 2005 and 2035. That improvement would occur mostly because the urban workforce is young. However, in the long run—between 2035 and 2050—the aging of the population would cause the finances of the system to deteriorate even if the entire formal sector participated in the pension plan. The study found, however, that the system could be sustainable and financially viable if retirement age is increased to 65 for both men and women (it is now 60 for men, 55 for women in salaried positions, and 50 for women in nonsalaried positions). Sustainability is possible only if the central government assumes the implicit debt of the system, Wang et al. contend.

Extending the working years of urban workers will require not only raising retirement ages but also government investment in lifelong learning so that China's over-55 population can continue to be a productive contributor to the economy. Changes in family structure—more young people wishing to form a nuclear family away from their parents, for example—might also prompt more of the "young old" to continue working in order to remain self-sufficient longer and build up savings for retirement. China "will have to have the mechanics in place" and be ready to provide the lifelong learning that could help older workers make a solid contribution to the economy, which could help blunt any negative economic impact of aging, Holzmann suggests.[85]

China's initial embrace of a partially funded system was based on its desire to avoid the vulnerability to aging that was so evident in some European social security systems. Some within the central government opposed and continue to oppose funded accounts. Their opposition became stronger in the aftermath of the Argentina crisis of late 2001 and early 2002, when the value of assets in Argentina's funded pension system plunged overnight and have only slowly and partially recovered. During 2002, as equity markets around the world experienced sharp declines, some within the State Council—in its Development Research Center and its Office for Restructuring the Economic System—argued that any new reform should rely mostly or entirely on a pay-as-you-go system. Some within the central government—in the Department of Distribution and Social Security System at the Office for Restructuring the Economic System—are arguing that "if France, which is an aging country, can rely on a generous pay-as-you-go system, then so can China," notes Zhang Xinmei. Zhang notes that this remains a minority, but strongly held, view.[86]

Worries about the viability of a social security system with a second tier of fully funded individual accounts appear to be driven by concerns about China's immature financial markets, which are seen as a challenge to achieving good returns on assets in the individual accounts. Many fear that the value of those funds could evaporate overnight in a financial crisis. Additional concern exists that if social security bureaus collect funds in these accounts and turn over the investment decisions to provincial financial departments—which has happened in some instances—the decisions on which government bond investments to make with these funds could be driven by political considerations or even corruption. Interests of the plan participants might not be paramount in investment decisions. The biggest concern, however, is locating investments that can provide a return at least equal to the rate of salary increases.

Even former staunch supporters of funded accounts such as Ge Yanfeng of the State Council's Development Research Center have become wary of the potential of funded accounts.[87] Ge worries about the immaturity of China's financial markets. In time, he suggests, China's markets will mature as long-term investors bring discipline to share prices. He argues, however, that the market could not handle a sudden surge of investments from pooled individual accounts.

Ge also thinks that the current basic guarantee of 20 percent of salary in the pay-as-you-go tier is too small for an optimum social security system.[88] After considerable study, Ge now favors reform that would create in China a system similar to that in the United States. That is, it would have a pay-as-you-go benefit providing approximately 40 to 45 percent of basic pay, as does the U.S. Social Security system. This benefit would be supplemented by employer-sponsored plans that could be either defined benefit or defined contribution plans. In either case, decisions about investing the money in the plans would be made by professional asset managers, not social security bureaus or provincial financial departments. Because an employer-sponsored plan would develop slowly, it could develop in concert with China's financial markets and, in fact, strengthen and deepen the markets, Ge argues.

The government also needs to end political interference in the operations of SOEs and let them sink or swim on their own. Selling them to the private sector can help, but China will also need to reform its bankruptcy laws to allow for quick resale of assets to new investors and clearly establish property rights for the owners of the former SOEs, argues Gary H. Jefferson, a professor of international trade and finance at Brandeis University.[89] This would allow assets of mammoth SOEs to be broken up and sold separately to investors who would be able to put them to profitable use.

One important element in moving China's economic growth path forward is to find the best way to continue to reform the pension system and still minimize the burden on enterprises in the midst of a transition to a new economic model. More workers must be moved into the highly productive sectors and mechanisms must be created to promote sharing among the populace the overall productivity increases accruing to the society. This includes continuing the effort to pool pension contributions, develop common benefits and funding mechanisms and to improve portability, and ensure that individual accounts are, in fact, funded. Current efforts at the provincial levels move in this direction, but they may not be enough. The aggregation of efforts at the provincial level is intended to allow greater mobility across firms and more equitable sharing of costs. As the society becomes more mobile, however, subaggregation at the provincial level may potentially inhibit workers' mobility as well as the cost sharing that will allow the greatest leveraging across the whole economy.

Notes

1. It is natural and to be expected that the rate of savings will decrease in the decades ahead.

2. Martin Feldstein, "Social Security Pension Reform in China," Working Paper no. w6794 (Cambridge, Mass.: National Bureau of Economic Research, November 1998), www.nber.org/papers/w6794.

3. Mao Yushi, "The Macroeconomic Implications of Pension Reform in China."

4. State Council Document 26.

5. Yaohui Zhao, "Perverse Pension Incentives," *Asian Wall Street Journal*, November 21, 2001, p. 6.

6. Data from the MLSS cited by Song Xiaowu, "China's Social Security System and Old-Age Pension Funds" (paper presented at the Asian Development Bank Annual Meeting, Shanghai, May 8–12, 2002), table 1, p. 5.

7. *China Statistical Yearbook 2002*, table 5-1. In 2000, there were 231.51 million urban employed persons; 106 million were counted in the social security system in 2001, or about 45.8 percent.

8. Data on the composition of China's workforce list all the categories for urban workers except government and military. If all the groups in the 2001 data are totaled, it leaves 62.86 million.

9. The 1997 reforms were codified in State Council Document 26, and the 2000 reforms were codified in State Council Document 46.

10. *Zhongguo 2000 nian renkou pucha ziliao* 1: 47, 76.

11. Ibid, p. 105.

12. *China Statistical Yearbook 2003*, p. 123.

13. Data from MLSS cited by Song Xiaowu, "China's Social Security System and Old-Age Pension Funds," a paper presented at the Asian Development Bank Annual Meeting in Shanghai, China, May 8–12, 2002.

14. *China Statistical Yearbook 2001*, table 5-1.

15. Ibid., table 10-17.

16. Ibid.

17. *China Statistical Yearbook 2003*, table 5-1.

18. Ibid.

19. OECD, *China in the World Economy*, figure 4.3, table 2.3, p. 89.

20. Ibid., chap. 4.

21. Philip Martin and Jonas Widgreen, "International Migration: Facing the Challenge, *Population Bulletin* 57, no. 1 (March 2002): 1–40.

22. "Funding the social safety net," *Asia Today*, June 2002.

23. Ibid.

24. 84.7 billion yuan or $10.23 billion based on an exchange rate of 8.27815 on October 2002.

25. "China's State-Owned Enterprise Lay-Offs Finding New Jobs: Minister," *People's Daily*, October 27, 2002, http://english.peopledaily.com.cn.

26. Ibid.

27. Xinhua News Agency, "Finance Minister says China to Continue to Increase Spending on Poverty Relief," April 16, 2002.

28. "Xiang Huaicheng's Report," *People's Daily*, March 4, 2002, http://english.people.com.cn.

29. Social spending of 98.2 billion yuan ($11.86 billion) for various social welfare measures includes 34.9 billion yuan ($4.22 billion) to subsidize the old-age insurance fund, and 31 billion yuan ($3.74 billion) to replenish the national social security. In addition, social spending includes 13.6 billion

yuan ($1.64 billion) for basic living allowances for laid-off workers from SOEs, 2.3 billion yuan ($278 million) for subsistence allowances for poor urban residents, and 8.4 billion yuan ($1.01 billion) for disabled military service members and their families and for other social welfare and relief funds. Currency conversions are based on an exchange rate of 8.27815 on October 25, 2002.

30. Benefits amounted to 86 billion yuan, reported from Beijing by Xinhua News Agency, "Finance Minister says China to continue to increase spending on poverty relief," April 16, 2002.

31. Data from China's MLSS cited on table 1, p. 5, of Song Xiaowu, "China's Social Security System and Old-Age Pension Funds" (paper presented at the Asian Development Bank Annual Meeting, Shanghai, May 8–12, 2002).

32. Kong Jingyuan, "Implicit Pension Debt and Its Repayment," in *Restructuring China's Social Security System*, ed. Wang Megkui, China Development Research Foundation Series (Beijing: Foreign Languages Press, 2002), pp. 175–176. Project to calculate the implicit debt was overseen by He Ping, deputy director of the Social Insurance Institute of the MLSS. The calculation for the implicit debt for 1995 was 1,317.428 billion yuan ($150 billion at the exchange rate of 8.27815 on October 2002), representing 22.5 percent of 1995's GDP of 5,847.81 billion yuan ($706 billion at the exchange rate of 8.27815 on October 2002).

33. Mark C. Dorfman and Yvonne Sin, "China: Social Security Reform, Technical Analysis of Strategic Options" (Washington, D.C.: World Bank, December 13, 2000), mimeo.

34. Kong Jingyuan, "Implicit Pension Debt and Its Repayment," p. 183. Estimated with 1996 data; percentages calculated for 1996 GDP.

35. Yan Wang, Dianqing Xu, Zhi Wang, and Fan Zhai, "Implicit Pension Debt, Transition Cost, Options and Impact or China's Pension Reform" (paper prepared for World Bank Policy Research Working Paper series and presented at a conference, "Developing through Globalization: China's Opportunities and Challenges in the New Century," July 5–7, 2000, Shanghai), p. 9, http://econ.worldbank.org/files/1416_wps2555.pdf.

36. Ibid.

37. Author's interview with Hu Feng Yun, former deputy director of the Shanghai Bureau of Social Security, Shanghai, September 24, 2002.

38. eFinancial News, "China sits on pension time bomb," August 12, 2002, www.efinancialnews.com.

39. Yan Wang et al., "Implicit Pension Debt, Transition Cost, Options and Impact or China's Pension Reform."

40. Ibid., p. 25.

41. Dorfman and Sin, "China: Social Security Reform, Technical Analysis of Strategic Options."

42. In constant 1995 yuan.

43. Yan Wang et al., "Implicit Pension Debt, Transition Cost, Options and Impact or China's Pension Reform."

44. 6 billion yuan ($725 million), 68 billion yuan ($8.214 billion), 115 billion yuan ($13.89 billion) based on an exchange rate of 8.27815 in October 2002.

45. Stuart H. Leckie, chairman of the Hong Kong Retirement Schemes Association, communication with author, January 3, 2004.

46. "Xiang Huaicheng's Report."

47. Social security spending of 34.9 billion yuan or $4.22 billion to subsidize the old-age insurance fund, and 31 billion yuan $3.74 billion to replenish the National Social Security Fund based on an exchange rate of 8.27815 on October 25, 2002.

48. David Murphy, "Pension Pinch," *Far Eastern Economic Review* (April 11, 2002): 48.

49. Reuters, "China allows foreign investment in listed firms," November 4, 2002.

50. "Pension fund seeks new investment channels," *China Daily* (Hong Kong edition), November 14, 2003.

51. Qixiang Sun and John W. Maxwell, "Deficits, Empty Individual Accounts, and Transition Costs: Restructuring Challenges Face China's Pension System," *Journal of Insurance Issues* 25, no. 2 (Fall 2002): 104, www.wria.org/JII/wriaabs/wriapdf/1F2002.pdf. The exchange rate was 8.27815 in October 2002.

52. OECD, *China in the World Economy*, figure 8.1, p. 278.

53. The family name is Zhao, which is normally placed first, ahead of the given name; however, some Chinese reverse the order, as Yaohui Zhao has done.

54. Yaohui Zhao, "Perverse Pension Incentives," *Asian Wall Street Journal*, November 21, 2001, p. 6.

55. Author's interview with Mu Huaizhong, a Liaoning University economics professor, September 18, 2002, in Shenyang; also Mu Huaizhong, *Zhongguo she hui bao zhang shi du shui ping yan jiu* (Studies on the proper level of social security in China) (Shenyang: Liaoning da xue chu ban she; Di 1 ban, 1998).

56. Calculated with the October 2002 exchange rate of 8.27815.

57. Author's interview with Zhang Xiao Long, economist with the Liaoning Provincial Social Insurance Administration Bureau, September 18, 2002.

58. Ibid.

59. "Pilot Social Security Program," *China Daily*, July 24, 2003.

60. Xinhua News Agency, "More Laid-Offs Benefit from China's Social Security Reform," 2002 (no specific date), posted by the Embassy of China in Canberra, Australia, www.chinaembassy.org.au (July 25, 2002).

61. Author's interview with Han Dongfang, Hong Kong labor activist, September 26, 2002. Han is a former railroad engineer who was arrested in 1989 after participating in protests at Tiananmen Square, where he was demanding rights for workers. He also formed Beijing Workers' Autonomous Federation, the only independent labor organization that briefly existed in China. He was jailed without charges and contracted tuberculosis in prison. After 22 months in jail, he was allowed to leave China for medical treatment. When he recovered (he lost one lung), he was not allowed to reenter China and has therefore remained in Hong Kong as a labor activist, even after Hong Kong came under the sovereignty of China.

62. See www.china-labour.org.hk.

63. Zhao and Xu, "Chinese Urban Pension System," 412.

64. Xinhua News Agency, "China Vows to Revitalize Northeastern Industrial Base," August 13, 2003.

65. "Business Booms in China's Gray Market," *China Daily*, December 28, 2003.

66. Yuan converted to the dollar at an exchange rate of 8.27815 (October 2002).

67. Qiao, "From Decline of Fertility to Transition of Age Structure," p. 78.

68. Elisabeth Rosenthal, "Without 'Barefoot Doctors,' China's Rural Families Suffer," *New York Times*, March 14, 2001, p. 1.

69. Pieter Bottelier, "Where Is Pension Reform Going in China? Issues and Options," *Perspectives* 3, no. 5 (June 2002), www.oycf.org/Perspectives/17_063002/Pension_China.htm.

70. Data reported by Zhang Zuoji, MLSS, speaking at a press conference at the Sixteenth Communist Party Congress, November 16, 2002.

71. Bottelier, "Where Is Pension Reform Going in China?"

72. Qiao, "From Decline of Fertility to Transition of Age Structure," pp. 77–78.

73. The State Council is the cabinet of the central government and is made up of the heads of the various ministries.

74. Chow, *Socialist Welfare With Chinese Characteristics*, p. 94.

75. Ibid., p. 17.

76. World Health Organization, "Country Profile: China," in *Global Tuberculosis Control*, (Geneva, Switzerland: World Health Organization, 2002), pp. 63–66.

77. Bates Gill, Jennifer Chang, and Sarah Palmer, "China's HIV Crisis," *Foreign Affairs* 81, no. 2 (March/April 2002): 96–110; also, Nicholas Eberstadt, "The Future of AIDS," *Foreign Affairs* 81, no.6 (November/December 2002): 22–45.

78. Sarah Cook, "After the Iron Rice Bowl: Extending the Safety Net in China," Discussion Paper 337 (Brighton, UK: University of Sussex, Institute of Development Studies, 2001).

79. *China Statistical Yearbook 2001*, p. 856.

80. United Nations Children's Fund (UNICEF), "UNICEF Statistics, China," February 1, 2002, www.unicef.org.

81. Gordon G. Liu, Peter Yuen, Tei-Wei Hu, Ling Li, and Zingshu Liu, "Urban Health Insurance Reform," Chapter 1 in *Urbanization and Social Welfare in China*, ed. Aimin Chen, Gordon G. Liu, and Kevin H. Zhang (Aldershot, Hampshire, UK: Ashgate Publishing Limited, 2002), p. 3.

82. Yaohui Zhao and Jianguo Xu, "Chinese Urban Pension System: Reforms and Problems," *Cato Journal* 21, no. 3 (Winter 2002).

83. Ibid., p. 41.

84. Wang et al., "Implicit Pension Debt, Transition Cost, Options and Impact or China's Pension Reform."

85. Ibid., November 27, 2002.

86. Author's interview with Zhang Xinmei, September 17, 2002.

87. Author's interview with Ge Yanfeng, deputy director general of the Department of Social Development at the State Council's Development Research Center, Beijing, September 20, 2002.

88. Liaoning's experiment provides a 30 percent benefit.

89. Gary H. Jefferson, "China's State-Owned Enterprises Did Their Job—Now They Can Go," *Transition Newsletter* 10, no. 5 (October 1999): 31–32.

5

An Aging China in a Global Economy

What future role will an aging China play in the global economy? In light of its changing demography, will China be able to develop successful programs for its urban and rural elderly? Will China's role be different from the role it plays today? Can China help mitigate the impact of aging in developed countries and at the same time improve its own prospects?

Financing Future Programs

A comprehensive study of the global financial and economic impact of aging by Kieran McMorrow and Werner Röger finds that China can improve its prospects while assisting other developed countries.[1] For developed countries in general, investment in developing countries can overcome the labor shortages of the developed countries. For the developing countries, the investment will help raise living standards. While China will also be aging rapidly during the next 50 years—more rapidly than the United States—the constant flow of people from rural areas into the cities will assure a constant supply of labor. To the extent that cross-border flows of capital and particularly FDI are unimpeded, developing nations can play a role in mitigating the economic drag that aging will bring to developed nations.

Funding the Implicit Pension Debt

A number of researchers have turned their attention toward how best to finance the implicit debt of the urban social security system. Yan Wang et al. proposed phasing out the current notional individual accounts and creating a funded account system by starting to fund the accounts of new employees according to the principle, "old people, old system; new people, new system."[2] Under this proposal, a new system would have three pillars: a small pay-as-you-go pillar, a transitional pillar, and a fully funded individual-account pillar.

The first pillar would be funded by 13 percent wage contribution from current and new workers. Only current workers in enterprises that are currently part of the system would contribute an additional 11 percent to finance preexisting pay-as-you-go benefits. The second pillar would also be partly funded by government subsidies. This pillar would be phased out as prereform retirees and current workers retire and die. The third pillar would be financed by contributions at levels that workers would determine on their own. Wang et al. found that the subsidies required in this approach would be reasonable: an estimated 0.5 to 0.6 percent of GDP during 2001–2035, falling thereafter to reach 0.3 percent in 2050.

The viability of adopting a policy of separately financing the implicit debt with central government bonds depends on the ability of China to assume new debt. China, with a very low 16 percent debt-to-GDP ratio, appears to be in a good official position to take on new debt. However, that 16 percent figure does not include contingent liabilities, such as the cost of pension and unemployment insurance reforms and the cost of restructuring the banking system. Jun Ma of Deutsche Bank and Fan Zhai of the Ministry of Finance in Beijing considered these contingent liabilities and estimated that they could amount to 65 percent of GDP over the next 50 years.[3] This includes 23 percent of GDP for the interest and principal on the bank restructuring bonds net of asset recovery from bad loans over the next 11 years. It also includes 41 percent of GDP for government subsidies to cover the costs of pension reform for a funded system, as proposed by Wang, to cover transition costs not paid by current workers.[4] It includes 1 percent of GDP for subsidizing unemployment insurance over the next 11 years. Absent any changes in tax policies, the government debt-to-GDP ratio will rise steadily to 62 percent in 2015, Ma and Zhai claim.

Ma and Zhai believe the Chinese government is unlikely to sit back and do nothing while its debt continues to rise. The government has, in fact, formulated plans to reform the tax system. Ma and Zhai predict that provisions likely to find favor include an expansion of the coverage of the consumption tax and the value-added tax, a reduction in corporate tax concessions, and a modest increase in income taxes. With these new tax measures and the reforms proposed by Wang et al., China should be able to manage the fiscal transition, and its debt-to-GDP ratio should rise no higher than 35 percent in 2015,[5] Ma and Zhai conclude.

The new pension reforms would, however, have to attract full participation of China's urban formal sector, and China's provinces would have to make enormous progress in integrating social security funds on a provincial level. These changes are unlikely to happen quickly and, thus, estimates based on a complete change overnight are, by definition, on the optimistic side. Further, because government subsidies are already rising faster than predicted by the 2000 model of Wang et al., the costs of transition could also be higher.

Funded Accounts and the Development of China's Financial Markets

China's financial markets have higher turnover than those of developed countries and are subject to speculation and manipulation. If individual accounts were fully funded and asset managers were allowed to invest in securities, the entry of large institutional investors focused on the long term would both deepen and stabilize the financial markets.[6] Since the design of China's pension reform of 1995 established individual funded accounts as the largest source of retirement income, it is important that the accounts earn a good rate of return if today's workers are to enjoy retirement security in the future. If returns are poor, the pensions drawing from individual accounts will be inadequate, and workers will get more retirement income from the unfunded basic pension than from the funded individual-account pension. Good returns on the funds in the individual accounts can assure that China can avoid handing huge new fiscal burdens to future generations of workers. If funds from individual accounts were to be invested in low-return bank accounts only, they would not grow large enough to provide the projected replacement income levels at retirement.

Government bonds offer a better prospect, especially as China develops longer-term bonds with higher yields.[7] Investments in government bonds must be made with the sole interest of the plan participant in mind. Local jurisdictions should not be permitted to bring pressure on local social security bureaus to invest in infrastructure that the local authorities cannot fund through taxes.

Workers will also need to be sure they earn a good return on retirement savings made through the third pillar of voluntary private sector benefits. To ready itself for employer-sponsored plans that are separate from the social security system, China will have to be prepared to regulate the investments of those plans to assure they are made in the best interests of plan participants. China, therefore, will need its own version of the Employee Retirement Income Security Act (ERISA), adopted in 1974 in the United States. Such a law in China would require that investments be made in the best interests of plan participants by following the prudent-investor principle; in other words, pension funds should set long-term investment goals and diversify their investments for the best risk-adjusted return. A draft pension regulation has been drawn up that would contain the kinds of protections found in ERISA.[8] If Chinese workers can accumulate their retirement savings under voluntary employer-sponsored plans—with assets managed by nonstate, independent asset managers—workers might gain a better return for themselves, a return generally free of the political influence that is sure to be brought to bear on the investment decisions of social security bureaus.

For several years, China has sought to determine the best way to bring the kind of maturity to its markets that it needs if pension funds are to be invested successfully in equities and in government and corporate bonds. One solution is to allow experienced fund managers from countries outside China to bring long-term, value-investing disciplines into the market. In November 2002—during the Sixteenth Party Congress—the China Securities Regulatory Commission and the People's Bank of China jointly released a circular that stated that beginning on December 1,

2002, foreign investors would be allowed to invest in listed A shares on the Shanghai and Shenzhen stock exchanges.[9] The new policy—the Qualified Foreign Institutional Investors (QFII) Scheme—had been in the works for several years. Before this change in policy, the A share market, denominated in yuan, was open only to domestic investors; foreigners could invest in B shares, denominated in U.S. and/or Hong Kong dollars.[10] The announcement of the QFII scheme followed by a few days an announcement that foreign investors could purchase nontradable state-held shares in SOEs. The new policy requires foreign investors to set up a special renminbi account with a domestic bank, which acts as custodian for the funds, and to use domestic securities companies for trading. Also, China will still maintain foreign exchange quotas for transferring capital into and out of the investment accounts of the foreign firms that participate in the QFII. According to the circular, foreign investment firms may acquire no more than 10 percent of the shares in a listed domestic firm. To participate in the scheme they must have five years' experience and must have managed at least $10 billion in assets in the prior year.

The QFII program is patterned after one that was set up in Taiwan a decade earlier, according to Anthony Neoh, a senior adviser to the China Securities Regulatory Commission since 1998.[11] Neoh predicts that until share prices in the Shenzhen and Shanghai markets reflect more clearly the values of the companies listed, it will be tricky for pension funds to invest in the stock market in China. Share prices in Shanghai and Shenzhen have been as high as 58 times earnings, and some firms with a tiny profit have traded at 13,000 times earnings while very profitable firms with solid prospects might trade at 5 times earnings. The markets do not have many sophisticated investors beyond the QFIIs, whose presence is so new they have not yet made an impact on the market. "Taiwan solved this problem 10 years ago by bringing in sophisticated Western institutional investors," Neoh commented, although he noted that Taiwan's markets are still volatile. He expects that the QFII program, although not a panacea, can stabilize China's markets.

If China continues on its track of starting to fund individual accounts, those accounts are likely to remain pooled accounts invested by local social security bureaus. Time will need to pass before large numbers of workers are able to make investment decisions about their retirement savings through the employer-sponsored third pillar of the retirement system. Nevertheless, 5 million workers are in enterprise annuities; but these have yet to offer the kinds of investments that are available in funded account systems in Hong Kong and Singapore. China's policymakers are watching to see how the Hong Kong Mandatory Provident Fund functions in that city's far more developed markets. They are also monitoring Singapore's Central Provident Fund.

Foreign companies remain hopeful that they will be able to enter China's pension markets. China's domestic insurance companies currently offer group plans to enterprises. In 2009 that policy will change to include foreign insurers, as China comes into compliance with WTO provisions. The investment management departments of insurance companies could also eventually be allowed to manage the individual account assets that are pooled at the local or provincial level on behalf of the social security bureaus. If both foreign and domestic insurance companies are able to offer group insurance products, it would help generate a huge retirement market worth 7.8 trillion yuan ($942 billion) in assets in 2020,[12] according to an analysis by Xiaoping Wu et al.[13] The market would be divided into two parts: 4.1 trillion yuan ($495 billion) in assets from individual accounts (the second pillar) and 3.7 trillion yuan ($447 billion) assets from enterprise annuities from group pension policies (the third pillar). By 2050 assets could hit 18.4 trillion yuan ($2.2 trillion), Wu at al. predict.

Although for a long time it seemed it would never happen, in the spring of 2003—more than 18 months after it received authorization—the National Social Security Fund began to invest up to 40 percent of its assets in stocks and mutual funds, up to 10 percent in corporate and Treasury bonds, and the rest in bank deposits. China's National Council of the Social Security Fund (NCSSF) has oversight of social security assets, estimated to be $133 billion yuan ($16 billion) in late 2003.[14] In 2002, the fund reported a 2.75 percent return on its assets, an increase over the 2.25 percent earned in 2001. By the end of 2003, NCSSF had invested only 5 percent of its assets in stocks. The stock market, however, declined in the second half of 2003, following poor corporate profits. The poor performance prompted criticism of the council and the six managers who invest its funds. The disappointment with equities has prompted the NCSSF to look for other investment opportunities outside stocks, bonds, and bank deposits. Potential investments include insurance products, trusts, overseas securities, and large infrastructure projects although such investments would require a change in the NCSSF's charter.

Investment in China

McMorrow and Röger note that the global economy has returned to a high level of capital integration that was seen before World War I. Unlike the pre-1914 world, however, the mobility of labor today is less than it was then.[15] "[T]he growth in FDI flows can at least partially be seen as a type of substitute for labor flows," the authors write.[16] If European nations, Japan, and the United States limit labor mobility and immigration that provides needed labor, it will become more important to the global economy and to the prospects for both developed and developing nations that FDI flows increase into fast-aging countries, like China, as well as slow-aging countries, like India.

China will have its own reasons for pursuing FDI, which not only helps develop the country but also prepares the country to deal with its aging population. David Hale believes that China's aging will in fact drive the country to further embrace capitalism: "[W]ith a low birthrate and an aging population, China in the future will have to generate adequate returns on its savings to provide income for its large retired population."[17]

Typical FDI entering China advances the state of productivity in a given business sector by only a couple of years, still many years behind the level of efficiency achieved in the advanced nations. To the extent that capital invested in surplus Chinese labor yields genuine improvements in productivity, it will generate real savings in China that can be can be deployed to help finance the legacy costs of the urban social security system, believes Sylvester Schieber, director of research for Watson Wyatt Worldwide.[18] Such improvements can also help raise living standards in China.

China and other developing nations need to embrace policies that allow foreign investment to earn a good return. This, in turn will attract the substantially higher FDI levels that are needed to benefit the economy, McMorrow and Röger contend.[19] "The world needs more not less globalization," to bring the needed benefits to developed and developing countries and counter the impact of aging, according to McMorrow.[20]

China, however, has engaged in policies that have hampered FDI, Schieber contends.[21] China has required Chinese partners in joint ventures, which makes it difficult to manage the enterprise efficiently so that it earns the kind of return that investment in a developing country should be expected to earn, Schieber explains. Foreign investors also need to be able to repatriate their investment: "If all the capital invested by foreigners gets locked up in China, and people can't get value in return, they'll invest somewhere else," Schieber says.[22]

China's own needs for investment are so great that China is unlikely to be an important source of global capital to be lent abroad when savings rates decline in developed nations, Schieber comments. Japan, on the other hand, will likely continue to hold great amounts of capital and be unable to get attractive returns from investing in its own economy. China needs Japan's surplus capital, and Japan needs China's surplus labor. Americans and Europeans with capital will also be looking for places to invest to achieve higher returns to offset lower returns associated with population aging at home. "Give every man in China a hammer and think what more they can do," Schieber says. China's contribution to the world in the era of aging, he adds, will be to provide goods and services to the people of Germany, Italy, Spain, Japan, and, to some extent, the United States—countries that will no longer have the labor forces they need to produce the goods they need.

China's Investment Abroad

China may also send some capital into developed countries instead of attracting it, a shift that could happen if China fails to improve the investment climate for its domestic private enterprises. If China establishes a regulatory regime that allows its funded pension schemes to invest some of their assets overseas, institutional investors may want to invest overseas in global companies that have growth opportunities to diversify their risks. China could allocate some of its pension funds to investment in foreign bonds if return is high enough, and it could provide buyers for equities from developed countries. If China's individual accounts are fully funded and supplemental employer pensions become popular, China could have considerable funds to invest—as much as $1 trillion by 2020 and $2.2 trillion by 2050.[23] This will not, however, be a panacea for the impact on financial markets in the developed world of China's aging. The demand for foreign equities from Chinese institutional investors, though perhaps not sufficient to fully offset the decline in demand for equities within the developed countries after 2025, could dampen the effect. Pension funds in the United States, the United Kingdom, Japan, Switzerland, and the Netherlands in approximately 2025 might begin dumping equities into the market to raise funds to pay benefits and reposition their portfolios to increase their investments in bonds to better match their liabilities and assets.[24] China's investors could dampen the effect on equities, however, by adding more purchasers on the demand side.

Prudent management of China's assets would initially limit China's overseas investments to a modest portion of assets. Eventually, however, there should be a full involvement of institutional investment inside and outside of China. The impact on any one nation would, however, likely be muted by the fact that China would diversify its foreign investments across the developed world, concentrating on where it could find appropriate returns.

The Bottom Line

Aging will add significantly to the burden of China's already costly transition to a developed country with a market economy. China's economic transition carries great risks for social upheaval and economic setbacks as the country adopts policies that reduce the extensive protection enjoyed by urban workers since the People's Republic was founded in 1949. Chinese officials are keenly aware of the challenges they face and are thoughtfully searching for the right balance of policies and the right ordering of priorities to assure success in the transitions that are going on now, as well as the big population shift slated to begin after 2010.

Barring economic, financial, and social policy missteps by the central government, China potentially has the resources to transition to a moderately developed country by the 2020s. Rapid aging, although it begins in 2010, is unlikely to be a significant damper on the economy and probably will not prevent China from emerging as world economic superpower with a significant middle class. After 2020, however, China will have more difficulty attaining its goal of moving toward the standards of living of the most developed nations, which its leaders optimistically expect to occur by 2050.

On the basis of current assumptions of fertility and the cost of the economic transition, the economic and possibly the fiscal burden of aging will become significant for China by the 2020s. China's aging burden could, however, be greater than expected because current assumptions in some key areas—the fertility rate, for example—may be optimistic. Most assumptions on the size of the population and the portion of the population that is elderly are based on a recovery in the currently low 1.5 total fertility rate. If China's fertility rate remains low, however, the burden of supporting its elderly will be far greater than currently imagined. In China, this will not lead to a labor shortage as in Europe because China will have a continuous supply of labor from the rural areas with their excess of redundant workers and continuing urbanization. China thus has the internal migration it will need to sustain its economic growth. The burden that will fall on future workers and the central government after the 2020s could be very heavy and in succeeding years could slow China's economy and as well as its gains in living standards.

The central government may have to assume a far greater financial burden than is currently envisioned as it takes steps to manage the potential burden of providing services to the elderly, especially those in the urban areas, where the elderly could constitute as much as 50 percent of the population in some cities.

The plight of the rural elderly will depend on a number of factors. If fertility rates recover, more sons will be born in rural areas than in urban areas and will be able to support elderly parents. As Qiao suggests, daughters, too, might begin to take on this burden. With so many children of rural China migrating to the cities, however, ties with parents left behind could be strained. To the extent that urban workers retain those ties to their rural parents, the rural elderly will have resources to sustain themselves in their old age.

In the long term, China's farmers of course need a pension system that will sustain them in their old age. A new pay-as-you-go system for rural China would immediately create an enormous new liability and pension deficit; because of this it is generally seen to be out of the question. It is also too late to get a funded system for farmers in place for all of rural China before the burden reaches a critical level in 2020s. Enrolling the hundreds of millions of nonagricultural workers in rural areas into either the urban social security scheme or a rural social security scheme will also be extremely difficult owing to the seasonal nature of rural work.

An additional question is how China will deal with the huge numbers of workers in the shadow economy. China in the future will likely have to provide direct welfare relief to the abjectly elderly poor, wherever they are—yet another financial burden on the Chinese state.

Bottelier noted that China's state assets are insufficient alone to meet the costs of the economic transition and to finance the implicit pension debt—let alone finance costs associated with welfare for the abjectly poor elderly. Thus, it is likely that China will have to borrow to close the gap. Because China begins with a low level of debt compared with the size of its economy, it has more room to borrow to meet its future needs and can spread the cost over many decades. The burden of aging need not, then, prevent the emergence of China as an economic superpower by the 2020s. It may instead be a spur to political leaders to pursue policies that will better prepare China for meeting the cost of caring for its huge elderly population.

Notes

1. Kieran McMorrow and Werner Röger, "Economic and Financial Market Consequences of Aging Populations," Economic papers no. 182 (Brussels: European Commission Directorate-General for Economic and Financial Affairs, April 2003).

2. Yan Wang, "China's Implicit Pension Debt and Financing Options," Washington, D.C., World Bank, October 19, 2001, p. 6.

3. Jun Ma and Fan Zhai, "Financing China's Pension Reform," paper presented at the conference on Financial Sector Reform in China," Harvard University, Cambridge, Mass., September 11–13, 2001, mimeo., p. 11.

4. Ibid., p. 12.

5. Ibid., p. 13.

6. Estelle James, "How Can China Solve Its Old Age Security Problem? The Interaction Between Pension, SOE and Financial Market Reform" (paper prepared for conference on financial sector reform in China, Harvard University, September 2001), www.estellejames.com/downloads/china.pdf.

7. Author's interview with Mark Dorfman, senior pensions economist in the World Bank's East Asian Human Development Unit, on the evolving bond market in China, September 11, 2002.

8. Author's interview with Ge Yanfeng, economist in the State Council Development Research Center, Beijing, September 20, 2002.

9. "Foreign Investors Greenlighted to Trade A Shares in China," *China Daily*, November 8, 2002.

10. Some domestic Chinese investors had legal access to invest in B shares through Hong Kong securities firms, however.

11. Author's interview with Anthony Neoh, senior adviser to the China Securities Regulatory Commission since 1998 and former chairman of the Hong Kong Securities and Futures Commission, Hong Kong, September 26, 2002.

12. With an exchange rate of 8.27815 as of October 2002.

13. Xiaoping Wu, Yingning Wei, Zhenghuai Li, Anping Fu, August Chow, "The Demography of Aging in China and Its Implications for Old Age Pension," April 2000, p. 23, www.actuaries.ca/meetings/aging/Chow.pdf. Xiaoping Wu served as vice chairman of the China Insurance Regulatory Agency.

14. "Pension Fund Seeks New Investment Channels," *China Daily*, November 14, 2003.

15. Ibid., p. 22.

16. Ibid.

17. Dave Hale, "The Outlook for China Policy," January 15, 2003, www.chinaonline.com/commentary_analysis/C03011537.asp.

18. Author's interview with Sylvester Schieber, director of research for Watson Wyatt Worldwide, November 27, 2002.

19. McMorrow and Röger, "Economic and Financial Market Consequences," p. 63.

20. Author's interview with Kieran McMorrow, May 24, 2003.

21. Author's interview with Sylvester Schieber, November 27, 2002.

22. Ibid.

23. Xiaoping Wu et al., "The Demography of Aging in China and Its Implications for Old Age Pension," p. 23.

24. England, *Global Aging and Financial Markets.*

Select Bibliography

Becker, Jasper. *Hungry Ghosts: China's Secret Famine*. New York: Free Press, 1997.

Bloom, David, and Jeffrey G. Williamson. "Demographic Transitions and Economic Miracles in Emerging Asia." *World Bank Economic Review* 12, no. 3 (September 1998): 419–455.

Bloomberg.com. "China's GDP Growth Seen Slowing in 2004 as State Curbs Lending." Bloomberg.com, December 23, 2003, http://quote.bloomberg.com/apps/news?pid=10000080&sid=aIOi7xeroAp0&refer=asia.

Bonin, John P., and Yiping Huang. "Foreign Entry into Chinese Banking: Does WTO Membership Threaten Domestic Banks?" Paper presented at City University of Hong Kong conference, "Greater China and the WTO," August 22–24, 2001.

Bottelier, Pieter. "Managing China's Transition Debt: Challenges for Sustained Development." Washington, D.C., November 7, 2002.

———. "Where Is Pension Reform Going in China? Issues and Options." *Perspectives* 3, no. 5 (June 2002), http://www.oycf.org/Perspectives/17_063002/Pension_China.htm.

Cai Fang, ed. *2002 nian Zhongguo ren kou yu lao dong wen ti bao gao: cheng xiang jiu ye wen ti yu dui ce* [2002 green book on the population and labor: employment in rural and urban China]. Beijing: She hui ke xue wen xian chu ban she [Chinese Academy of Social Sciences], 2002.

Cai Fang and Wang Meiyan. "How Fast and How Far Can China's GDP Grow?" *China & World Economy* 10, no. 5 (September–October 2002): 9–15, http://www.iwep.org.cn/wec/english/articles/2002_05/2002-5-caifang.pdf.

Cao Gui-Ying. "The Future Population of China: Prospects to 2045 by Place of Residence and by Level of Education." Singapore: National University of Singapore, Asian MetaCentre for Population and Sustainable Development Analysis, April 20, 2000.

Chang, Gordon G. "China's Banks: The Only Two Things You Need To Know." *China Brief* 2, no. 6 (Washington, D.C.: Jamestown Foundation, March 14, 2002), http://www.jamestown.org/publications_details.php?volume_id=18&&issue_id=646.

Chang, Gordon G. *The Coming Collapse of China.* New York: Random House, 2001.

Chang Tianle. "Bad Loans Back on the Agenda." *China Business Weekly,* November 25, 2003.

Chen Shengli. *The Mortality Changes of China since the 1930s.* Beijing: China Population Press, 1993.

China Business Weekly. "GDP No Longer Sole Index of Growth." December 16, 2003.

China Statistical Yearbook 2001, 2002, 2003. Beijing: National Bureau of Statistics of China, China Statistics Press, 2001, 2002, 2003.

China Statistics Press. "Data of 1995 One Percent Population Survey." Beijing: China Statistics Press, 1997.

"China's Local Trade Barriers: A Hard Nut to Crack." *Transition Newsletter* 12, no. 3 (July–August–September 2001), http://www.worldbank.org/transitionnewsletter/pdf/JulAugSep01Printable.pdf.

Chow, Gregory C. *China's Economic Transformation.* Malden, Mass.: Blackwell, 2002.

Chow, Nelson W. S. *Socialist Welfare with Chinese Characteristics: The Reform of the Social Security System in China.* Hong Kong: University of Hong Kong, 2000.

Dayal-Gulati, Anuradha, and Aasim M. Husain. "Centripetal Forces in China's Economic Takeoff." *IMF Staff Papers* 49, no. 3 (2002): 364–392, http://www.imf.org/External/Pubs/FT/staffp/2002/03/pdf/gulati.pdf.

Dorfman, Mark C., and Yvonne Sin. "China: Social Security Reform, Technical Analysis of Strategic Options." Washington, D.C.: World Bank, December 13, 2000.

Duncan, Fergus. "China's Banking Sector: An Uneven Playing Field." FinanceAsia.com, February 14, 2001, http://www.financeasia.com.

Eberstadt, Nicholas. "The Future of AIDS." *Foreign Affairs* 81 no.6 (November/December 2002): 22–45.

Eckholm, Erik. "Prenatal Scans Aid Chinese Couples to Abort Unwanted Girls." *International Herald Tribune,* June 23, 2002, p. 4.

Economist Intelligence Unit. "Country Briefings: China." Economist Intelligence Unit, http://www.economist.com/countries/china (October 30, 2002).

England, Robert Stowe. *The Fiscal Challenge of an Aging Industrial World.* Washington, D.C.: Center for Strategic and International Studies, 2002.

———. *Global Aging and Financial Markets: Hard Landings Ahead?* Washington, D.C.: Center for Strategic and International Studies, 2002.

———. *The Macroeconomic Impact of Global Aging: A New Era of Economic Frailty?* Washington, D.C.: Center for Strategic and International Studies, 2002.

Feldstein, Martin. "Social Security Pension Reform in China." Working paper no. w6794, Cambridge, Mass., National Bureau of Economic Research, November 1998, www.nber.org/papers/w6794.

Fischer, Gunther, Yufeng Chen, and Laixiang Sun. "The Balance of Cultivated Land in China during 1988–1995." Paper no. IR-98-047. Laxenburg, Austria: International Institute of Applied Systems Analysis, August 1998, http://www.iiasa.ac.at/Publications/Documents/IR-98-047.pdf.

Foo, Raymond, Tham Mun Hon, Winner Lee. "Behind the Bamboo Curtain." Hong Kong: BNP Paribas Peregrine, October 2002.

Forney, Matthew. "Workers' Wasteland." *Time International* 159, no. 12 (June 17, 2002): 40–44.

Gilboy, George, and Eric Heginbotham. "China's Coming Transformation." *Foreign Affairs* 80, no. 4 (July/August 2001): 26–39.

Gill, Bates, Jennifer Chang, and Sarah Palmer. "China's HIV Crisis." *Foreign Affairs* 81, no. 2 (March/April 2002): 96–110.

Hale, David. "The Outlook for China Policy." January 15, 2003, http://www.chinaonline.com/commentary_analysis/C03011537.asp.

He Zengke. "Fighting Corruption through Institutional Innovations toward Good Governance." Beijing: China Center for Comparative Politics and Economics, 2000.

Higgins, Matthew, and Jeffrey G. Williamson. "Age Structure Dynamics in Asia and Dependence on Foreign Capital." *Population and Development Review* 23 (June 1997): 261–293.

Huang Yasheng. *Selling China: Foreign Direct Investment during the Reform Era.* Cambridge: Cambridge University Press, 2003.

Hudson, Valerie M., and Andrea Den Boer. "A Surplus of Men, A Deficit of Peace: Security and Sex Ratios in Asia's Largest States." *International Security* 26, no. 4 (Spring 2002): 5–38, http://mitpress.mit.edu/journals/pdf/isec_26_04_5_0.pdf.

Hussain, Athar. "Social Welfare in China in the Context of Three Transitions." Working paper no. 66. Palo Alto, Calif.: Stanford University, Center for Research on Economic Development and Policy Reform, August 2000, http://credpr.stanford.edu/pdf/credpr66.pdf.

———. "Urban Poverty in China: Measurement, Patterns and Policies." Geneva: International Labor Organization, January 2003, http://www.ilo.org/public/english/protection/ses/download/docs/china.pdf.

Jackson, Richard. *The Global Retirement Crisis: The Threat to World Stability and What to Do About It.* Washington, D.C.: CSIS/Citigroup, 2002.

James, Estelle. "How Can China Solve Its Old Age Security Problem? The Interaction Between Pension, SOE and Financial Market Reform." Paper prepared for conference on financial sector reform in China, Harvard University, September 2001, http://www.estellejames.com/downloads/china.pdf.

Jefferson, Gary H. "China's State-Owned Enterprises Did Their Job—Now They Can Go." *Transition Newsletter* 10, no. 5 (October 1999): 31–32.

Kong Jingyuan. "Implicit Pension Debt and Its Repayment." In *Restructuring China's Social Security System*, edited by Wang Megkui. China Development Research Foundation Series. Beijing: Foreign Languages Press, 2002.

Kraay, Aart. "Household Saving in China." *World Bank Economic Review* (September 2000), http://www.worldbank.org/research/bios/akraay/Household%20Saving%20in%20China.pdf.

Krugman, Paul. "The Myth of Asia's Miracle." *Foreign Affairs* 78, no. 6 (November/December 1994): 62–78.

Leckie, Stuart H. *Pension Funds in China.* Hong Kong: ISI Publications, January 1999.

Leckie, Stuart, and Tony Zhang. *Investment Funds in China.* Hong Kong: FinanceAsia.com, 2001.

Lin Jiang. "Changing Kinship Structure and Its Implications for Old Age Support in Urban and Rural China." *Population Studies* 49, no. 1 (1995): 127–145.

———. "Parity and Security: A Simulation of Old-Age Support in Urban and Rural China." *Population Development Review* 20, no. 2 (1994): 423–448.

Liu, Gordon G., Peter Yuen, Tei-Wei Hu, Ling Li, and Zingshu Liu. "Urban Health Insurance Reform." Chapter 1 in *Urbanization and Social Welfare in China,* edited by Aimin Chen, Gordon G. Liu, and Kevin H. Zhang, 1–22. Aldershot, Hampshire, UK: Ashgate Publishing Limited, 2002.

Lu Xueyi, ed. *Dangdai Zhongguo shehui jieceng yanjiu baogao* [Research report on social strata in contemporary China]. Beijing: Shehui kexue wenxian chubanshe [China social sciences publishing house], 2001.

Ma Jun and Fan Zhai. "Financing China's Pension Reform." Paper prepared for conference on financial sector reform in China, Harvard University, September 2001.

Mao Yushi. "The Macroeconomic Implications of Pension Reform in China." Paper presented at China Center for Economic Research/Cato Institute conference, *China's Pension System: Crisis and Challenge*. Beijing, November 8, 2001.

Martin, Philip, and Jonas Widgreen. "International Migration: Facing the Challenge." *Population Bulletin* 57, no. 1 (March 2002): 1–40.

McMillan, Alex Frew. "China Growth Myths Dispelled." CNN Asia, October 30, 2002.

McMorrow, Kieran, and Werner Röger. "Economic and Financial Market Consequences of Aging Populations." Economic papers no. 182. Brussels: European Commission Directorate-General for Economic and Financial Affairs, April 2003.

Mu Huaizhong. *Zhongguo she hui bao zhang shi du shui ping yan jiu* (Studies on the proper level of social security in China). Shenyang: Liaoning da xue chu ban she; Di 1 ban, 1998.

Murphy, David. "Nothing More To Lose." *Far Eastern Economic Review* 165, no. 30 (November 7, 2002): 30–32.

Murphy, David. "Pension Pinch." *Far Eastern Economic Review* 165, no. 14 (April 11, 2002): 48.

Nam, Yong-Sook. "Overview of Industry Prospects." Chapter 4 in *China in the World Economy*. Paris: OECD, 2002.

O'Donnell, Lynne. "Chinese Crisis in Gender Ratio." *The Australian*, May 14, 2002, World section, p. 8.

Organization for Economic Cooperation and Development (OECD). *China in the World Economy*. Paris: OECD, 2002.

People's Daily. "80 Million Jobs Created in Past 13 Years, Prospects Brighter." November 12, 2002, http://english.peopledaily.com.cn/other/archive.html.

Pitsilis, Emmanuel, David A. von Emloh, and Yi Wang. "Filling China's Pension Gap." *McKinsey Quarterly*, no. 2 (March 22, 2002): 20.

Rawski, Thomas G. "What's Happening to China's GDP Statistics?" *China Economic Review* 12, no. 4 (December 2001): 298–302.

Reutersward, Anders. "Labour Market and Social Benefit Policies." Chapter 16 in *China in the World Economy* (Paris: OECD, 2002).

Ru Xin, Lu Xueyi, and Shan Tianlun, eds. *2001 Shehui lanpishu: zongguo shehui xingshi fengxi yu yuce* [Social blue book 2001: an analysis and forecasting of social conditions in China]. Beijing: Shehui kexue wenxian chubanshe, 2001.

Sito, Peggy. "Managers Sought for Mainland Nest Egg." *South China Morning Post*, September 25, 2002, p. 1.

Song Xiaowu. "China's Social Security System and Old-Age Pension Funds." Paper presented at the annual meeting of the Asian Development Bank, Shanghai, May 8–12, 2002.

Standard & Poor's. *Asia-Pacific Banking Outlook 2004.* Hong Kong: Standard & Poor's, September 2003.

Standard & Poor's. *China Banking Outlook 2003–2004.* Beijing: Standard & Poor's, June 2003.

Standard & Poor's. *China Financial Services Outlook 2004.* Hong Kong: Standard & Poor's, November 2004.

Sun, Qixiang, and John W. Maxwell. "Deficits, Empty Individual Accounts, and Transition Costs: Restructuring Challenges Face China's Pension System." *Journal of Insurance Issues* 25, no. 2 (Fall 2002): 104, http://www.wria.org/JII/wriaabs/wriapdf/1F2002.pdf.

Takayama Noriyuki. "Pension Reform of PRC: Incentives, Governance and Policy Options." Paper prepared for the Fifth Anniversary Conference on Challenges and the New Agenda for the People's Republic of China, Asian Development Bank, December 5–6, 2002, Tokyo.

Turner, Dave, Claudio Giorno, Alain De Serres, Ann Vourc'h, and Peter Richardson. "The Macroeconomic Implications of Aging in a Global Context." Economics Department working paper no. 193. Paris: OECD, 1998.

United Nations (UN), Population Division, Department of Economic and Social Affairs. *World Population Ageing 1950–2050.* New York: UN, 2002.

———. *World Urbanization Prospects: The 2001 Revision.* New York: UN, 2002.

Waldron, Arthur. "China's Disguised Failure." *Financial Times,* July 4, 2002, Comment and analysis section, p. 17.

Walker, Meredith M., and Richard Alm. "China's Churn." Dallas: Federal Reserve Bank of Dallas, September 2000, http://www.dallasfed.org/research/pubs/churn.pdf.

Wang, Yan. "China's Implicit Pension Debt and Financing Options." Washington, D.C.: World Bank, October 19, 2001.

Wang, Yan, Dianqing Xu, Zhi Wang, and Fan Zhai. "Implicit Pension Debt, Transition Cost, Options and Impact or China's Pension Reform." Paper prepared for World Bank Policy Research Working Paper series and presented at a conference, "Developing through Globalization: China's Opportunities and Challenges in the New Century," July 5–7, 2000, Shanghai, http://econ.worldbank.org/files/1416_wps2555.pdf.

Williamson, Jeffrey G. "Demographic Shocks and Global Factor Flows." In Conference series no. 46, *Seismic Shifts: The Economic Impact of Demographic Change,* edited by Jane Sneddon Little and Robert K. Triest, 247–269. Boston: Federal Reserve Bank of Boston, 2001, http://www.bos.frb.org/economic/conf/conf46/conf46h1.pdf.

World Bank. *East Asian Miracle: Economic Growth and Public Policy.* World Bank Policy Research Report. New York: Oxford University Press, 1993.

World Bank. *Old Age Security: Pension Reform in China.* Washington, D.C.: World Bank, 1997.

World Health Organization (WHO). "Country Profile: China." In *Global Tuberculosis Control.* Geneva: WHO, 2002.

Wu, Xiaoping, Yingning Wei, Zhenghuai Li, Anping Fu, and August Chow. "The Demography of Aging in China and Its Implications for Old Age Pension." April 2000, http://www.actuaries.ca/meetings/aging/Chow.pdf.

Xiaochun Qiao. "Aging Issue and Policy Choices in Rural China." Speech to the 24th International Union for the Scientific Study of Population, Salvador, Brazil, August 20–24, 2001.

———. "From Decline of Fertility to Transition of Age Structure: Ageing and Its Policy Implications in China." *Genus* 17, no. 1 (January–March 2001): 57–81.

Xinhua News Agency. "Job Assistance for Laid-off Workers Sweeps China." July 21, 2002.

Yuying, Mark, An Wei Li, and Dennis Tao Yang. "Great Leap Forward or Backward? Anatomy of a Central Planning Disaster." Working paper no. 01-19. Charlottesville, Va.: Darden Graduate School of Business Administration, March 2001. http://papers.ssrn.com/sol3/papers.cfm?abstract_id=282526.

Zhao Yaohui, and Jianguo Xu. "Chinese Urban Pension System: Reforms and Problems." *Cato Journal* 21, no. 3 (Winter 2002).

Zhongguo 2000 nian renkou pucha ziliao [Tabulation of the 2000 population census of the People's Republic of China]. 3 vols. Beijing: China Statistics Press, August 2002.

Index

Page numbers followed by the letters n and t refer to notes and tables, respectively.

About the Author

Robert Stowe England has been a financial editor and journalist for more than 20 years. From 1999 to 2002, he served as director of research for the Global Aging Initiative at CSIS. England has written extensively on employee benefits, retirement, and pensions in a variety of journals and magazines and has written a number of research papers on retirement issues. He has also written often on business strategy, banking, corporate finance, the economy, and foreign affairs. He is the author of three studies for CSIS: *The Fiscal Challenge of an Aging Industrial World, Global Aging and Financial Markets: Hard Landings Ahead?* and *The Macroeconomic Impact of Global Aging: A New Era of Economic Frailty?* He is the chief author of *Safe and Sound: A 10-Year Plan for Promoting Personal Financial Security* (American Benefits Council, 2004). England has also been a featured speaker on aging issues at forums around the globe. Selections of his work can be found at http://www.robertstoweengland.com.